KATE GREENAWAY
Cross Stitch Designs
Julie Hasler

KATE GREENAWAY
Cross Stitch Designs

Julie Hasler

d&C

David & Charles

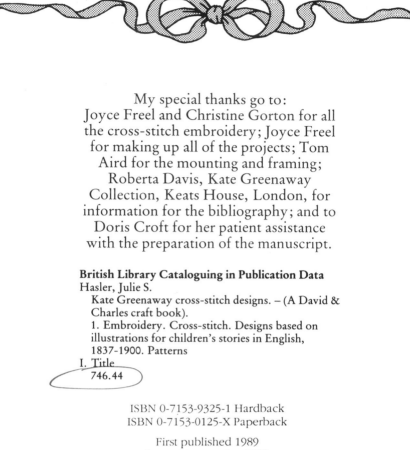

My special thanks go to:
Joyce Freel and Christine Gorton for all
the cross-stitch embroidery; Joyce Freel
for making up all of the projects; Tom
Aird for the mounting and framing;
Roberta Davis, Kate Greenaway
Collection, Keats House, London, for
information for the bibliography; and to
Doris Croft for her patient assistance
with the preparation of the manuscript.

British Library Cataloguing in Publication Data
Hasler, Julie S.
  Kate Greenaway cross-stitch designs. – (A David &
Charles craft book).
  1. Embroidery. Cross-stitch. Designs based on
illustrations for children's stories in English,
1837-1900. Patterns
  I. Title
  746.44

ISBN 0-7153-9325-1 Hardback
ISBN 0-7153-0125-X Paperback

First published 1989
Second impression 1989
Third impression 1990
First published in paperback 1993

Photographs by Di Lewis

Typeset by ABM Typographics Ltd, Hull
and printed in West Germany
by Mohndruck GmbH
for David & Charles   Newton Abbot   Devon

Distributed in the United States by
Sterling Publishing Co Inc,
387 Park Avenue South, New York, NY 10016-8810

CONTENTS

KATE GREENAWAY
(1846–1901)
Page 6

INTRODUCTION
Page 8

GENERAL
DIRECTIONS
Page 10

LACE-TRIMMED
CUSHIONS
Page 16

COT QUILT
Page 28

FRAMED PICTURES
Page 56

LAVENDER BAGS
Page 76

GREETINGS CARDS
Page 81

MINIATURES
Page 86

TABLECLOTH
Page 92

JAM-POT COVERS
Page 97

TRINKET BOXES
Page 101

PAPERWEIGHTS
Page 104

NIGHTDRESS BAG
Page 107

CHILD'S SKIRT
Page 113

BIBLIOGRAPHY
Page 118

INDEX
Page 120

KATE GREENAWAY
(1846–1901)

Born in London in 1846, Kate Greenaway was a brilliant artist and illustrator, exhibiting her work at the Royal Academy from 1877. She had a very special gift for finding beauty in the things around her and for conveying this rose-tinted view of life and nature to others. Her drawings of both children and flowers were sensitively observed and executed with a fresh and delicate use of colour so that her work was praised by art critics throughout the world.

By the 1880s, Kate Greenaway had become the darling of the Victorians and her popular books were being produced in editions of over ten thousand. Her idyllic vision of

childhood was exquisitely translated into delicate drawings of children in high-waisted dresses and mob caps, romping blissfully in a world of sunshine and flowers. The innocence and charm of these illustrations captivated the public and each new book was eagerly awaited and discussed. Her drawings influenced fashion to such a degree that dressmakers designed childrens clothing in a style that the French were to call 'Greenawisme'.

Kate Greenaway died in 1901 but the beauty and liveliness of her work has had an enduring appeal. Her illustrations are still known and loved around the world today and indeed have inspired this collection of cross-stitch designs. Julie Hasler has translated some of the most enchanting Kate Greenaway illustrations into cross-stitch designs to decorate a wide variety of items. These will brighten up your home or make superb gifts for family and friends by recreating Kate Greenaway's world of old-fashioned charm.

INTRODUCTION

Cross-stitch is a very simple, versatile and elegant needlecraft – a rewarding and inexpensive hobby. Both experienced and inexperienced needleworkers will find projects in this book to suit their abilities. If you are a complete novice and have never attempted cross-stitch before, take care to read the next few sections thoroughly before you begin. Take your time. If you have difficulty in absorbing all the information at first, refer back to the relevant section to check the details. The section entitled 'Important Advice' on p14 will prove very helpful.

The designs illustrated in this book show many refreshing ways in which cross-stitch can be used to decorate the home, or to make children's clothes or unusual gifts. Included in the many projects are a set of four lace-trimmed cushions, a child's cot quilt, lavender bags, pictures, trinket boxes and a child's skirt. All the items are beautifully embellished with Kate Greenaway figures. Making up the projects has been made as simple as possible, with complete instructions given with each project. Anyone with a basic knowledge of needlework will be able to create these charming items. Given as presents to family and friends, your work will be appreciated much more than a gift you have bought. These hand-made gifts will have your own personal touch and will be treasured by the receiver for many years to come.

The projects may be worked by following the charts exactly or, by altering the colours or combining motifs from several projects, you can stitch your own designs. For example, you could take a few of the designs from the cot cover and make them up as framed pictures to hang in the nursery to complement the quilt, or you could take a figure from the child's skirt and embroider it on a blouse pocket to match. There are many applications for these designs. Experiment with your work and use your imagination to create your own exclusive designs.

GENERAL DIRECTIONS

The charted designs in this book were originally created for counted cross-stitch, but they can easily be translated into other needlework techniques such as needlepoint, crochet and knitting, to name but a few.

In the counted-thread work, the finished piece of work will not be the same size as the charted design unless you are working with canvas or fabric which has the same amount of threads per inch as the chart has squares per inch.

The size of the finished piece of work will vary with crochet and knitting according to the number of stitches per inch.

MATERIALS

NEEDLES
A small blunt tapestry needle, No 24 or No 26.

FABRIC
Even-weave fabrics are used for cross-stitch such as Aida, Hardanger and Ainring. The type of fabric to be used is given with each project.

THREADS
The charted designs in this book have been keyed to shades of DMC stranded cotton, which is six stranded. The amount of strands used in the work will depend on the fabric used. Details of this are given with each project.

EMBROIDERY HOOP
For cross-stitch, it is best to use a 10, 13 or 15cm (4in, 5in or 6in) round wooden or plastic hoop with a screw-type tension adjuster.

SCISSORS
A pair of sharp embroidery scissors is essential, especially if a mistake has to be cut out.

PREPARING TO WORK

The following steps will allow you to achieve a much better coverage of your fabric.

To prevent the fabric from ravelling, the edges can either be covered with a fold of masking tape, or whip-stitched or machine-stitched. It is important where you make the first stitch, as it will place the finished design on your fabric. Find the exact centre point of the chart by following the arrows to their intersection . Locate the centre of the fabric by folding it in half vertically and then horizontally, pinching along the folds. The centre stitch of the chart will be where the creases in the fabric meet. Mark along these lines with basting stitches if necessary (see p15).

It is preferable to begin cross-stitch at the top of the design. To locate the top, count the squares up from the centre of the chart, then count left or right to the first symbol. Count the corresponding number of holes up and across from the centre of the

fabric and begin at that point. Remember that each square on the chart represents a stitch to be made on the fabric.

Place the fabric in the embroidery hoop, gently pull it taut and tighten the screw. You will find it easier to have the screw in the '10-o-clock' position to prevent the thread from becoming tangled in the screw with each stitch. However, if you are left-handed, have the screw in the '1-o-clock' position. While working, you will find it necessary to continue retightening the fabric to keep it taut, as tension makes it easier to push the needle through the holes without piercing the fibres.

When working with stranded cotton, always separate the strands and place them together again before threading your needle and beginning to stitch. Always use separate strands, never double thread. For example, if you need to use two strands, use two separate strands, not one doubled up.

METHOD

To make the stitch, bring the needle up from the wrong side, through a hole in the fabric (see Fig 1) at the left end of a row of stitches of the same colour. Fasten the thread by holding a short length of thread on the underside of the fabric and secure it with the first two or three stitches as

in Fig 2. Never knot your thread as this will create a bumpy back surface and prevent your work from lying flat when it is finished. Next bring the needle across one block (or square) to the right and one block above on a left to right diagonal as in Fig 1. Half the stitch is now

Fig 1

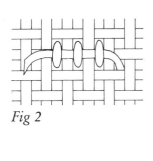

Fig 2

completed. Continue in this way until you reach the end of the row. Your stitches will be diagonal on the right side of the fabric and vertical stitches on the wrong side. Complete the stitch by crossing back from right to left to form an X as in Fig 3. Work all the stitches in the row by completing the Xs as in Fig 4.

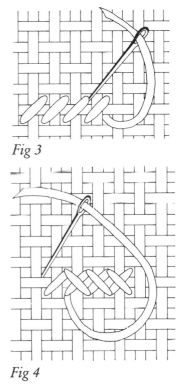

Fig 3

Fig 4

Cross-stitch can also be worked by crossing each stitch as you come to it, as you would do for isolated stitches. This method works just as well – it is really a personal preference. Vertical

rows of stitches are worked as shown in Fig 5.

Fig 5

Backstitch is used for outlines, face and hand details etc. It is worked from hole to hole and can be stitched in horizontal, vertical or diagonal lines as shown in Fig 6.

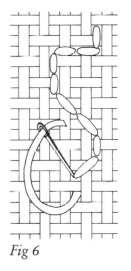

Fig 6

Finish all threads by running your needle under four or more stitches on the reverse side of your work as in Fig 7 and cut close.

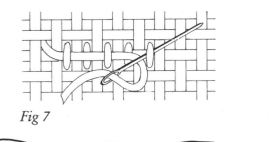

Fig 7

IMPORTANT ADVICE

1 When stitching, be careful not to pull the fabric out of shape. Work the stitches in two motions, straight up through a hole in the fabric and then straight down ensuring that the fabric remains taut. Do not pull the thread taut – it should be snug, but not tight. Using this method, the thread will lie just where you want it to and will not pull your fabric out of shape.

2 If the thread becomes twisted during working, drop the needle and let it hang down so that it untwists by itself. Twisted thread will appear thinner and will not cover the fabric as well.

3 Do not leave the needle in the design area of your work when it is not in use. No matter how good the needle might be, it may rust in time.

4 When carrying thread from one area to another, finish off and begin again. Do not carry thread across an open expanse of fabric. Loose threads, especially dark colours, will be visible from the front of your work when the project is completed.

5 Backstitch is worked when the cross-stitch embroidery has been completed. Always use one strand less than that used in the embroidery. For example, if you have used three strands of stranded cotton to work the cross-stitch embroidery, use two strands for the backstitching. If one strand of stranded cotton is used to work the cross-stitch embroidery, one strand is also used for the backstitching. Always take care not to pull the backstitches too tight, otherwise the contrast of colour will be lost against the cross-stitches.

6 When you have completed the cross-stitch embroideries, you may need to press them. To protect the embroideries when you press them, place them right side down onto a soft towel and cover the reverse side with a slightly damp cloth.

STITCHES USED

RUNNING STITCH
Running stitch is short and closely spaced, giving the illusion of an unbroken line. Use a thread that matches your fabric. To avoid tangling, use a single thread no more than 50cm (19½in) long. The stitches should be fine, approximately 2mm (⅛in) long and evenly spaced on both the top and reverse sides. When you become familiar with this stitch, your working speed can be increased by picking up several stitches on the needle before pushing it through.

Running stitch

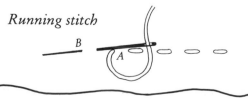

BASTING/TACKING STITCH

Basting or tacking stitches are also sewn by hand. They are used temporarily to hold layers of fabric, lace, wadding, etc, in a particular position. The stitches are removed once the project is complete. Use a contrasting colour of thread that is easy to see.

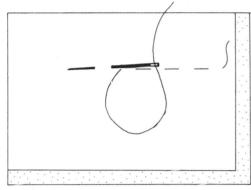

Basting/tacking

OVERSEWING

Working from right to left, bring the needle out of the fabric just above the edge. Insert the needle below, making a horizontal stitch to the left. Place the needle back into the hole it came out of and make a diagonal stitch up and to the left.

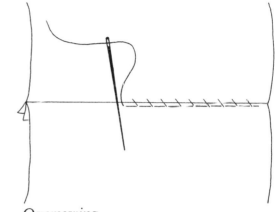

Oversewing

WHIP STITCH

Whip stitch over the edge of your fabric using double strands of thread to match the fabric. The stitches should be evenly spaced, no more than 6mm (1/4in) apart. Fasten the end of the thread with a knot.

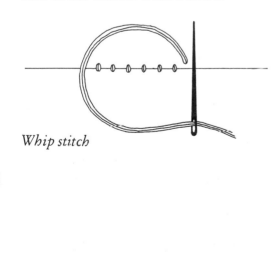

Whip stitch

SLIP STITCH

Slip stitching is used to join two pieces of fabric together by hand and gives an almost invisible finish. Insert the needle at A, slide 4-7mm (1/8-1/4in) through the folded edge of the fabric and bring out at B. Directly below B, make a small stitch through the second piece of fabric.

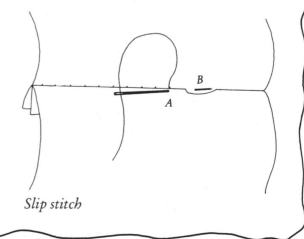

Slip stitch

LACE TRIMMED CUSHIONS

These beautiful lace and satin cushions are simple to make and will brighten up any room. Each one has a slightly different border and its own central design: Lamb, Duck, Two Maids and Young Lady with Dog. They make a charming set.
(Charts 1–4)

MATERIALS

For each cushion you will require:
1m (39in) cream satin
1.20m (47½in) frilled lace 76mm (3in) wide
1 cushion 38 x 38cm (15 x 15in)
1 19cm (7½in) square of cream Ainring with 18 stitches to the inch
DMC 6-strand stranded cotton
Sewing thread to match the fabric

All measurements include a 1cm (½in) seam allowance.

DIRECTIONS

1 Complete the cross-stitch embroidery using two strands of the stranded cotton.

2 From the cream satin, cut pieces as follows:
Back: 1 piece 40 x 40cm
  (15¾ x 15¾in)
Sides: 2 pieces 12.5 x 19cm
  (5 x 7¾in)
Top and bottom: 2 pieces 12.5 x 40cm
  (5 x 15¾in)

3 Sew each side piece to the central embroidered square and press the

seams to the sides. The diagram shows the finished sizes of all pieces, after seam allowances have been taken.

4 Sew the top and bottom pieces in place and press the seams outwards.

5 Cut the lace into four strips each measuring 30cm (11¾in). Join these strips together, starting to stitch 5cm (2in) from the cut edge and slanting to a point at the outer edge of the lace as shown in Fig 1. Trim off any excess lace.

6 Place the lace square onto the

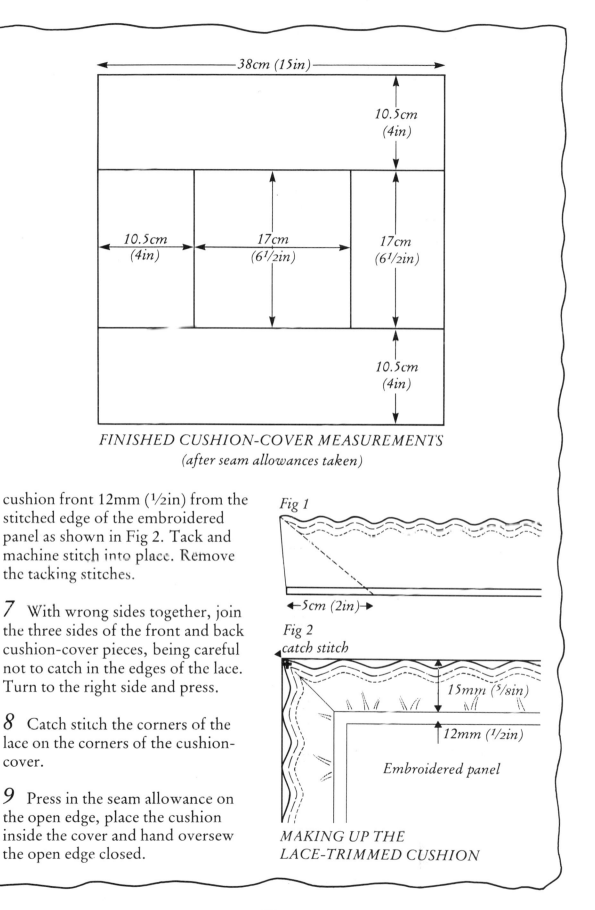

38cm (15in)

10.5cm (4in)

10.5cm (4in)   17cm (6½in)   17cm (6½in)

10.5cm (4in)

FINISHED CUSHION-COVER MEASUREMENTS
(after seam allowances taken)

cushion front 12mm (½in) from the stitched edge of the embroidered panel as shown in Fig 2. Tack and machine stitch into place. Remove the tacking stitches.

7 With wrong sides together, join the three sides of the front and back cushion-cover pieces, being careful not to catch in the edges of the lace. Turn to the right side and press.

8 Catch stitch the corners of the lace on the corners of the cushion-cover.

9 Press in the seam allowance on the open edge, place the cushion inside the cover and hand oversew the open edge closed.

Fig 1

←5cm (2in)→

Fig 2
catch stitch

15mm (⅝in)

12mm (½in)

Embroidered panel

MAKING UP THE
LACE-TRIMMED CUSHION

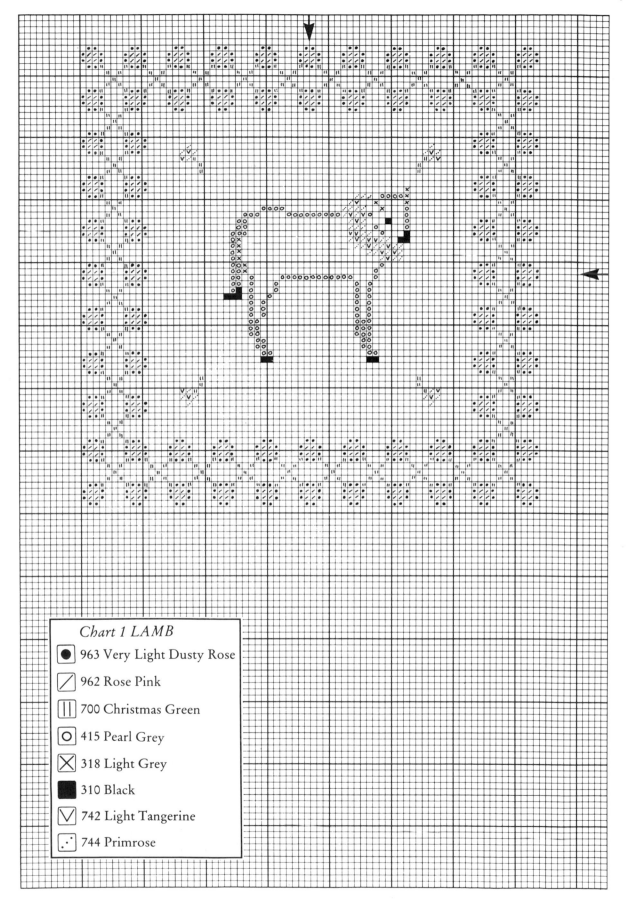

Chart 1 LAMB

●	963 Very Light Dusty Rose
╱	962 Rose Pink
‖	700 Christmas Green
○	415 Pearl Grey
✕	318 Light Grey
■	310 Black
V	742 Light Tangerine
∴	744 Primrose

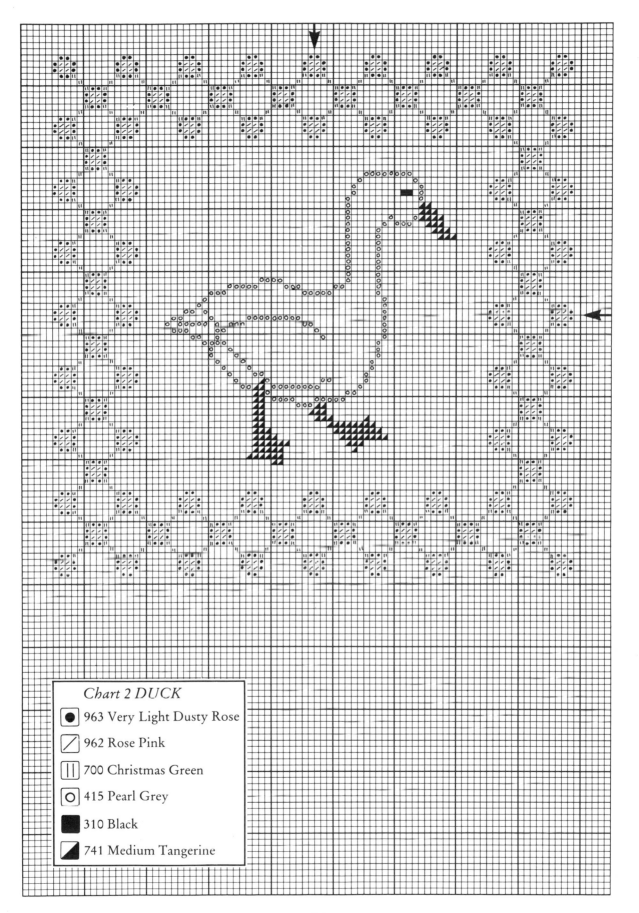

Chart 2 DUCK

●	963 Very Light Dusty Rose
∕	962 Rose Pink
‖	700 Christmas Green
○	415 Pearl Grey
◼	310 Black
◢	741 Medium Tangerine

LAMB

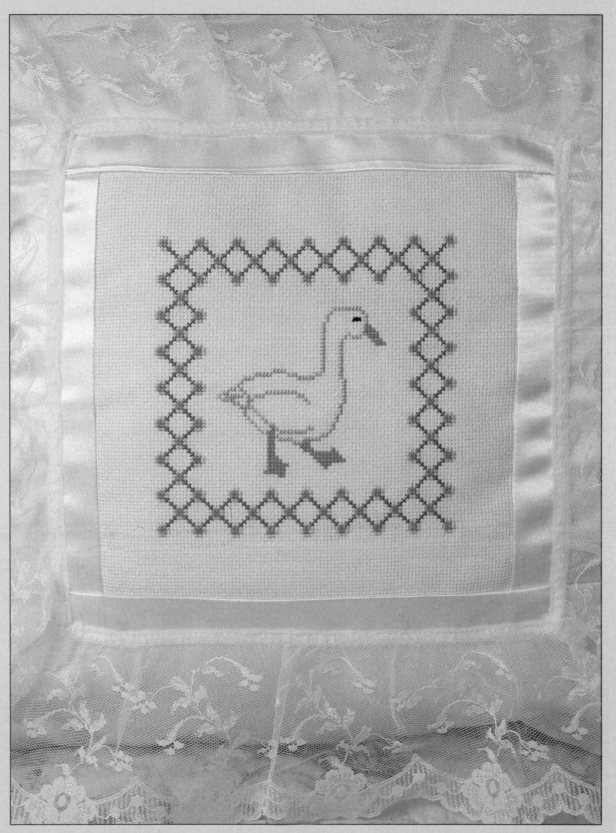

DUCK

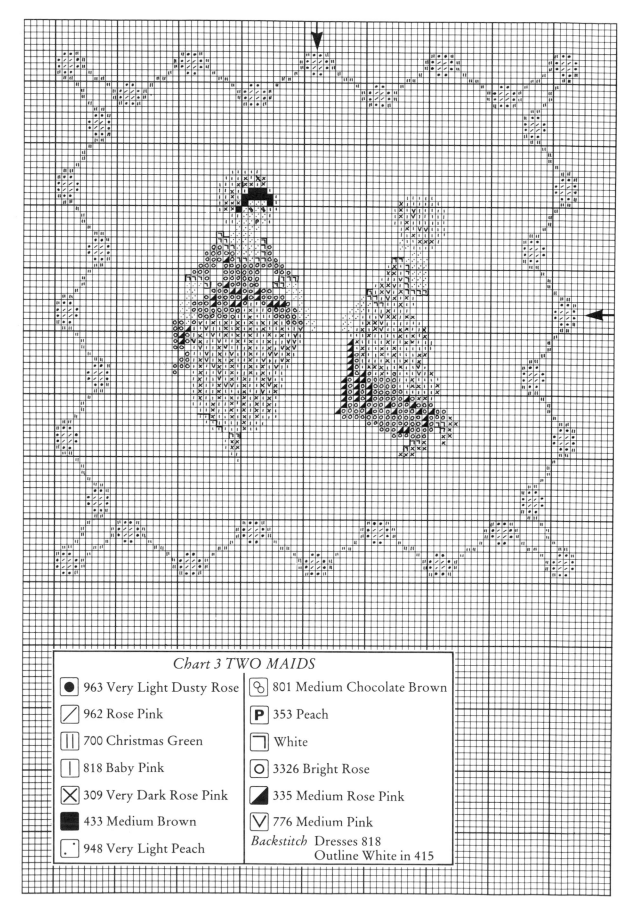

Chart 3 TWO MAIDS

Symbol	Color	Symbol	Color
●	963 Very Light Dusty Rose	⌀	801 Medium Chocolate Brown
╱	962 Rose Pink	P	353 Peach
‖	700 Christmas Green	⊓	White
│	818 Baby Pink	O	3326 Bright Rose
✕	309 Very Dark Rose Pink	◢	335 Medium Rose Pink
■	433 Medium Brown	V	776 Medium Pink
∴	948 Very Light Peach		

Backstitch Dresses 818
Outline White in 415

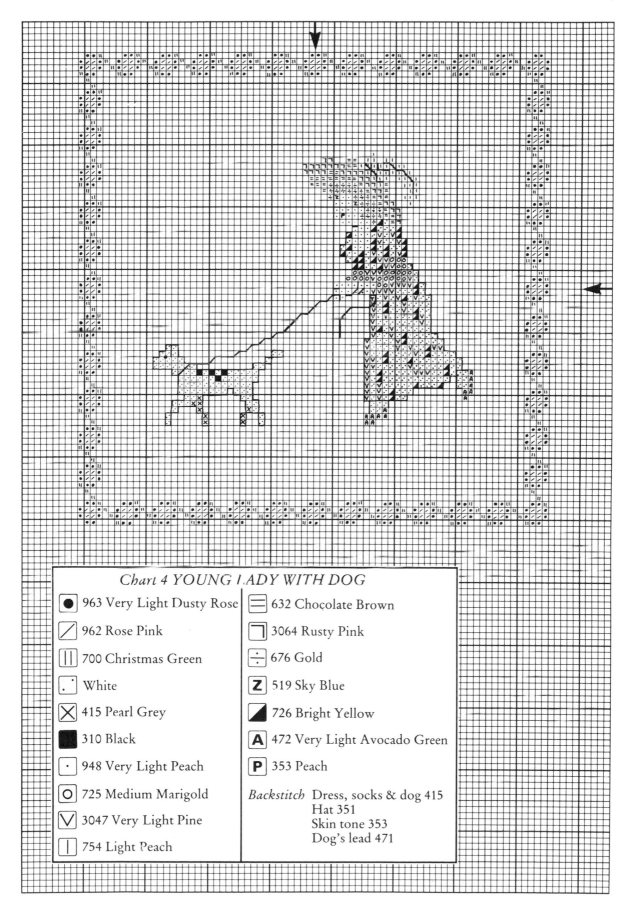

Chart 4 YOUNG LADY WITH DOG

●	963 Very Light Dusty Rose	⊟	632 Chocolate Brown
╱	962 Rose Pink	⊓	3064 Rusty Pink
‖	700 Christmas Green	÷	676 Gold
∴	White	Z	519 Sky Blue
✕	415 Pearl Grey	◣	726 Bright Yellow
■	310 Black	A	472 Very Light Avocado Green
·	948 Very Light Peach	P	353 Peach
O	725 Medium Marigold		
V	3047 Very Light Pine		
I	754 Light Peach		

Backstitch Dress, socks & dog 415
Hat 351
Skin tone 353
Dog's lead 471

TWO MAIDS

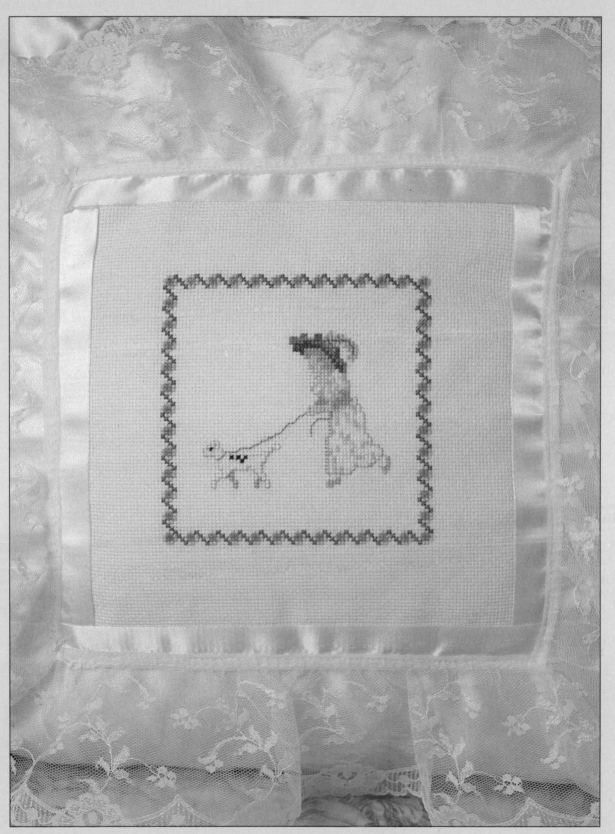

YOUNG LADY WITH DOG

COT QUILT

An embroidered quilt is a delightful addition to any child's room. The following directions are for making up the quilt exactly as shown in the photograph. You can alter the quilt to your own personal taste by altering the order of the embroideries on the quilt or by selecting three or four designs and arranging them to your choice. You can also change the colour of the borders and backing. For example, instead of using pink for a girl's room, as shown, you could use blue for a boy's room or a contrasting patterned or floral print. Whatever your choice, this beautiful quilt will give great pleasure for many years. (Charts 5–16)

MATERIALS

12 25 x 25cm (10 x 10in) squares of white fine Aida with 14 stitches to the inch. These measurements include 12mm (½in) seam allowance. When made up the square will measure 23 x 23cm (9 x 9in)
2m (78¾in) of 152cm (60in) wide fabric for backing and dividers
1.3m (51¼in) of wadding 1m (39½in) wide
DMC 6-strand stranded cotton
Sewing cotton to match the fabric

DIRECTIONS

Complete all your cross-stitch embroideries using two strands of stranded cotton and carefully press them.

Position the designs 1–12 as shown in the photograph of the finished quilt. For the backing and dividers, cut the fabric as follows (see Fig 1).

A: 8 pieces 9 x 25cm (3½ x 9¾in)
B: 3 pieces 9 x 85cm (3½ x 33½in)
C: 2 pieces 10cm x 1.15m (4 x 45¼in)
D: 2 pieces 10cm x 1.01m (4 x 39¾in)

E: 1 piece 1.01 x 1.31m (39¾ x 51½in)

These measurements include a seam allowance on all edges.
Assemble the quilt front as shown in Fig 2.

1 Sew the embroidered blocks and the vertical dividers (A) together to form horizontal strips.

2 Sew the horizontal strips and the horizontal dividers (B) together.

3 Add the sides (C).

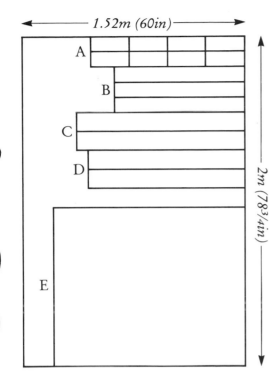

Fig 1 COT QUILT:
FABRIC CUTTING GUIDE

1.52m (60in)

2m (78³/₄in)

A
B
C
D
E

4 Finally add the top and bottom borders (D).

5 Press all the seams towards the squares.

Assembling the quilt
Lay the backing piece of fabric (E) right side down on a flat surface, placing the wadding on top.
Place the completed quilt front on top of the wadding right side up.
Ensure that all edges are even.
Pin and tack all the fabrics together around the squares.
Quilt around each square by hand, using small running stitches to penetrate all the layers. Remove the pins and tacking stitches.

FINISHING
Fold in a 6mm (¹/₄in) seam allowance on all the edges of the quilt front over the wadding. Tack in place. It may be necessary to trim the wadding slightly to avoid too much bulk at the edges.
Fold in a 6mm (¹/₄in) on all edges on the quilt backing.
Secure to front by tacking. Slip stitch all round, making sure that the stitches do not go through to the right side.

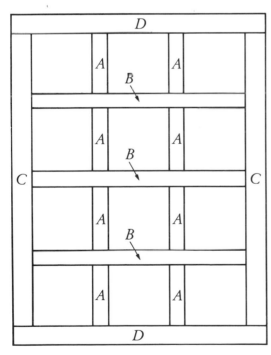

Fig 2 MAKING UP THE COT QUILT

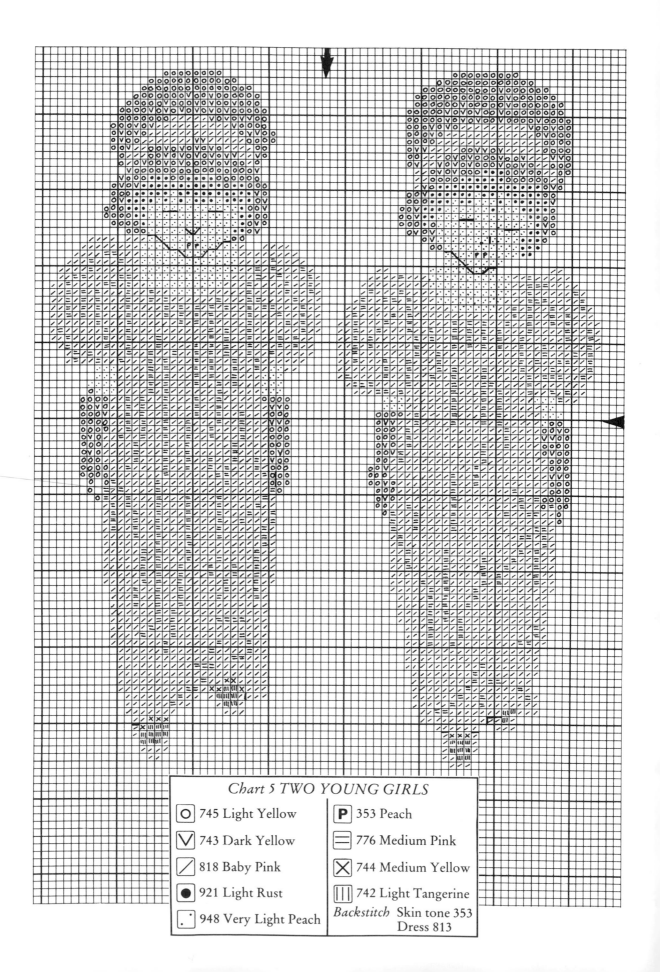

Chart 5 TWO YOUNG GIRLS

⊙	745 Light Yellow	P	353 Peach	
V	743 Dark Yellow	=	776 Medium Pink	
∕	818 Baby Pink	X	744 Medium Yellow	
●	921 Light Rust	⦀	742 Light Tangerine	
.	948 Very Light Peach		*Backstitch* Skin tone 353	
			Dress 813	

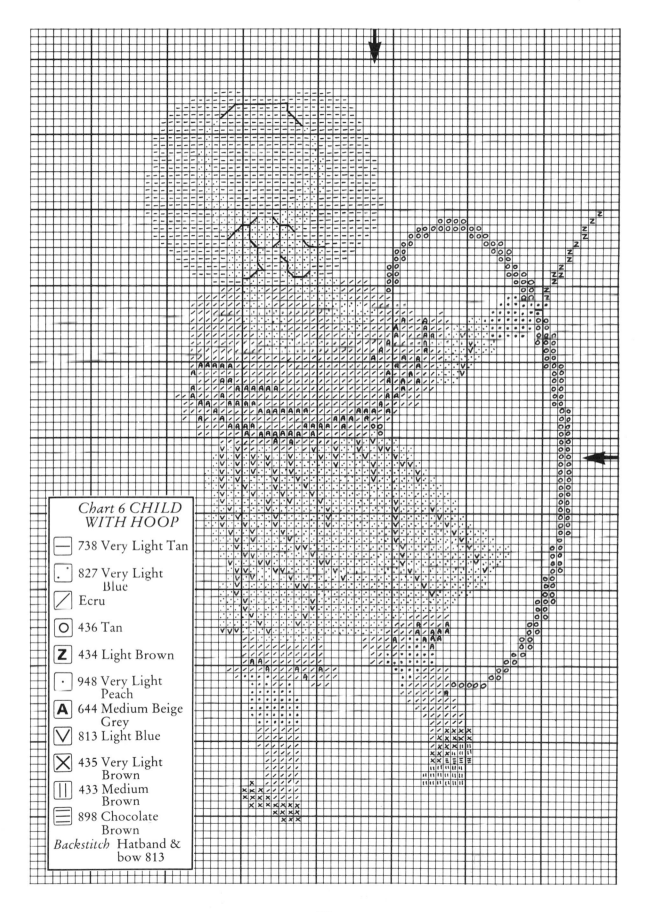

Chart 6 CHILD
WITH HOOP

─ 738 Very Light Tan

⋅ 827 Very Light
Blue

╱ Ecru

○ 436 Tan

Z 434 Light Brown

⋅ 948 Very Light
Peach

A 644 Medium Beige
Grey

V 813 Light Blue

X 435 Very Light
Brown

‖ 433 Medium
Brown

≡ 898 Chocolate
Brown

Backstitch Hatband &
bow 813

33

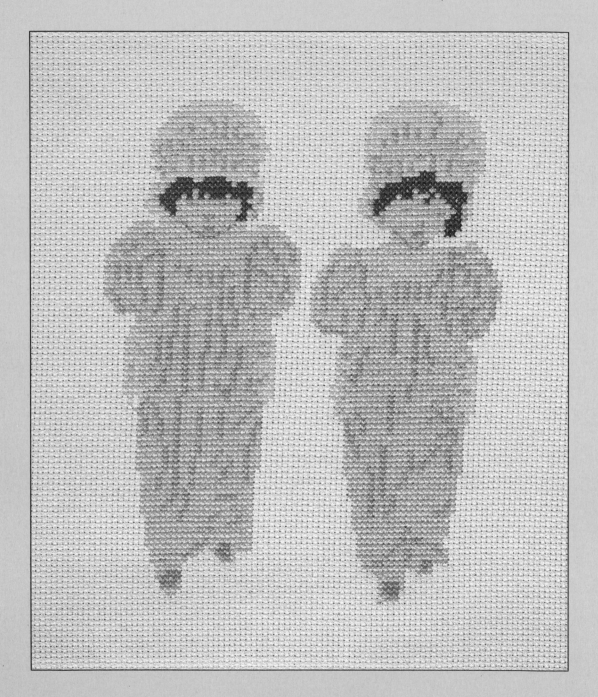

TWO YOUNG GIRLS

CHILD WITH HOOP

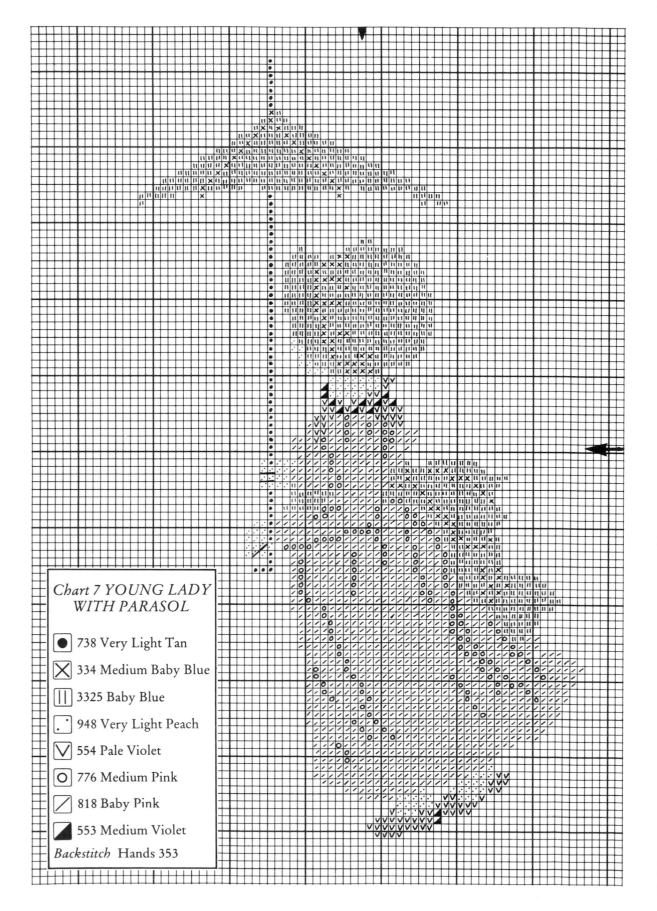

Chart 7 YOUNG LADY
WITH PARASOL

● 738 Very Light Tan

⊠ 334 Medium Baby Blue

‖ 3325 Baby Blue

∴ 948 Very Light Peach

V 554 Pale Violet

O 776 Medium Pink

╱ 818 Baby Pink

◣ 553 Medium Violet

Backstitch Hands 353

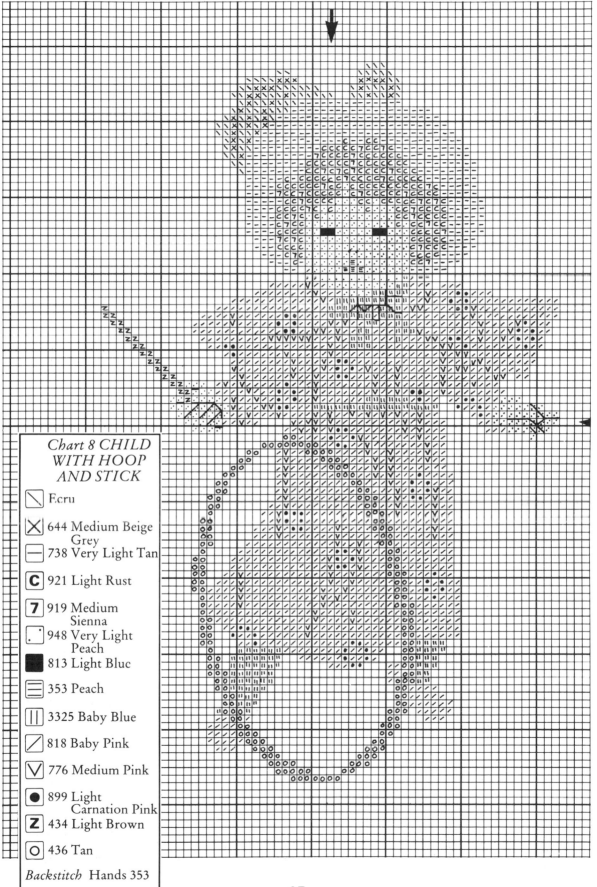

Chart 8 CHILD
WITH HOOP
AND STICK

⟍ F.cru

✕ 644 Medium Beige
Grey

— 738 Very Light Tan

C 921 Light Rust

7 919 Medium
Sienna

. 948 Very Light
Peach

█ 813 Light Bluc

≡ 353 Peach

‖ 3325 Baby Blue

╱ 818 Baby Pink

V 776 Medium Pink

● 899 Light
Carnation Pink

Z 434 Light Brown

O 436 Tan

Backstitch Hands 353

YOUNG LADY WITH PARASOL

CHILD WITH HOOP AND STICK

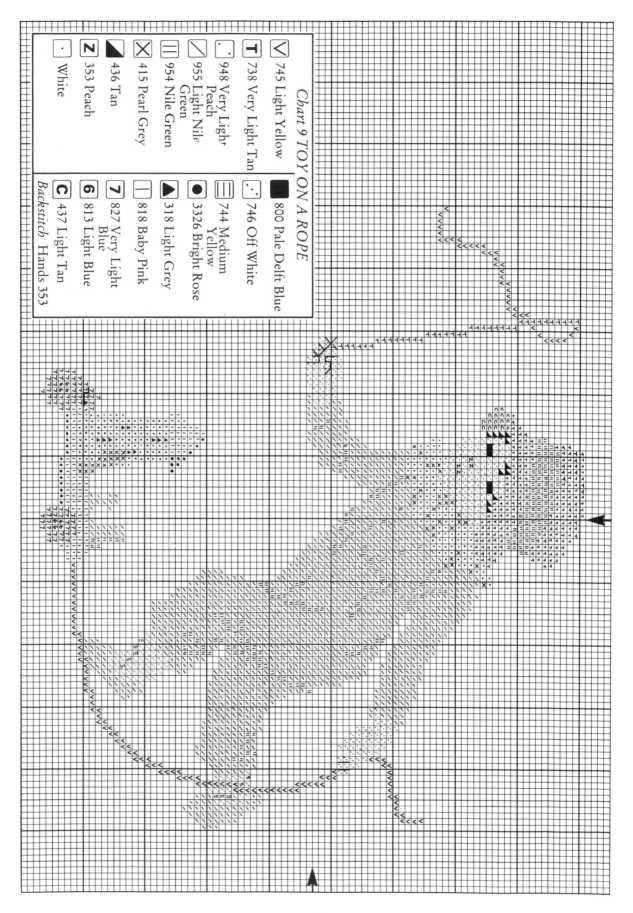

Chart 9 TOY ON A ROPE

V	745 Light Yellow
T	738 Very Light Tan
.	948 Very Light Peach
/	955 Light Nile Green
‖	954 Nile Green
X	415 Pearl Grey
▲	436 Tan
.	White

■	800 Pale Delft Blue
∴	746 Off White
≡	744 Medium Yellow
●	3326 Bright Rose
▶	318 Light Grey
		818 Baby Pink
7	827 Very Light Blue
6	813 Light Blue
C	437 Light Tan

Backstitch Hands 353

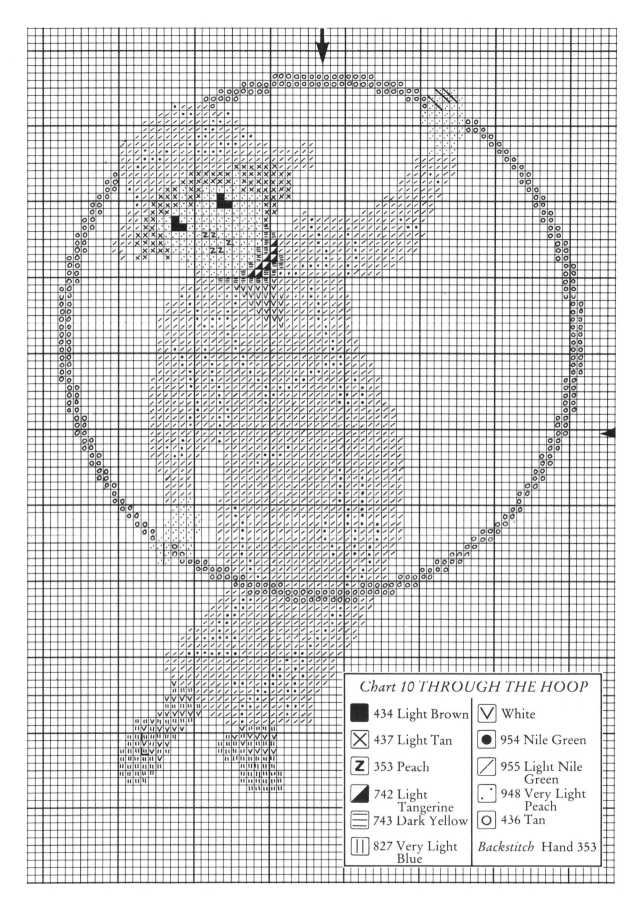

Chart 10 THROUGH THE HOOP

■	434 Light Brown	V	White
X	437 Light Tan	●	954 Nile Green
Z	353 Peach	/	955 Light Nile Green
◢	742 Light Tangerine	.˙	948 Very Light Peach
≡	743 Dark Yellow	O	436 Tan
‖	827 Very Light Blue	*Backstitch* Hand 353	

TOY ON A ROPE

THROUGH THE HOOP

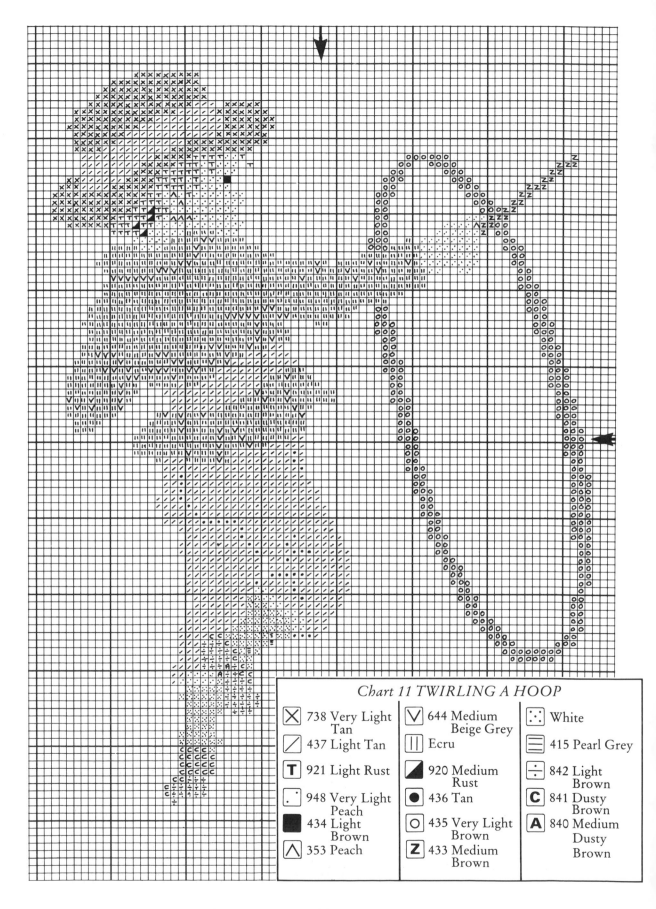

Chart 11 TWIRLING A HOOP

X	738 Very Light Tan	V	644 Medium Beige Grey	∴	White
/	437 Light Tan	‖	Ecru	≡	415 Pearl Grey
T	921 Light Rust	◣	920 Medium Rust	÷	842 Light Brown
.	948 Very Light Peach	●	436 Tan	C	841 Dusty Brown
■	434 Light Brown	O	435 Very Light Brown	A	840 Medium Dusty Brown
∧	353 Peach	Z	433 Medium Brown		

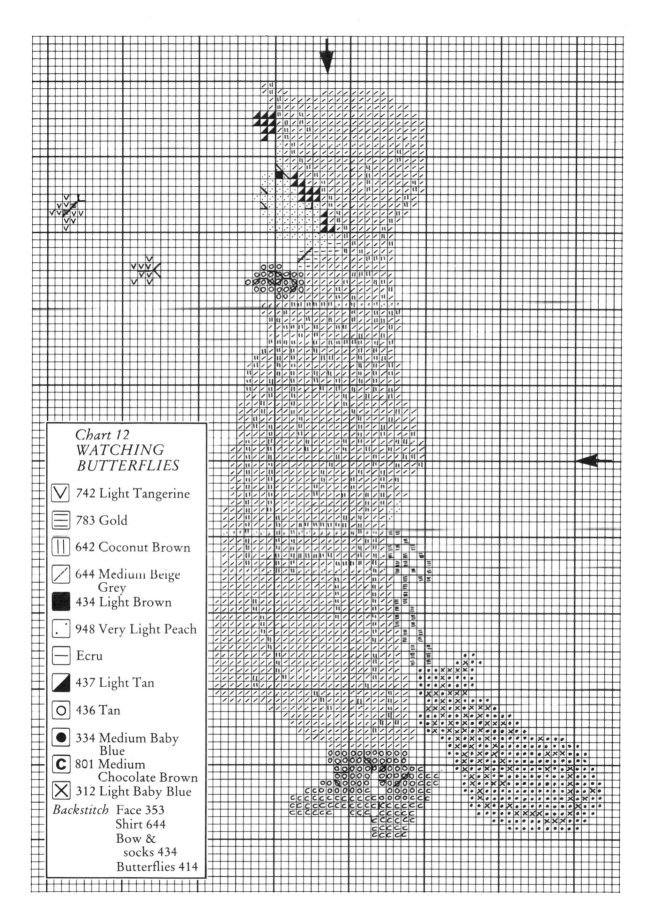

Chart 12
WATCHING
BUTTERFLIES

	742 Light Tangerine
≡	783 Gold
‖	642 Coconut Brown
/	644 Medium Beige Grey
■	434 Light Brown
.	948 Very Light Peach
—	Ecru
◢	437 Light Tan
O	436 Tan
●	334 Medium Baby Blue
C	801 Medium Chocolate Brown
X	312 Light Baby Blue

Backstitch Face 353
Shirt 644
Bow &
socks 434
Butterflies 414

TWIRLING A HOOP

WATCHING BUTTERFLIES

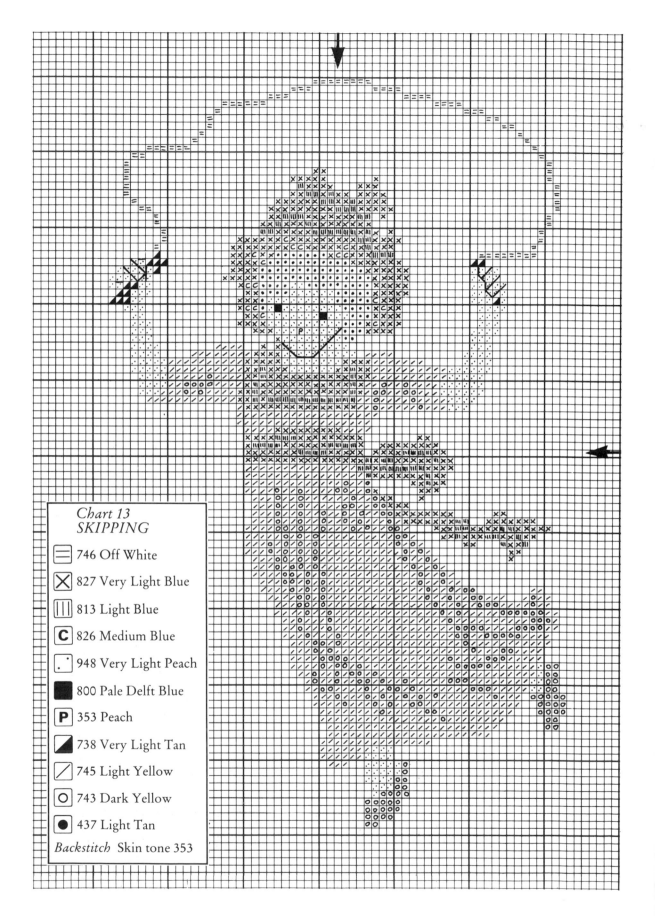

Chart 13
SKIPPING

⊟	746 Off White
✕	827 Very Light Blue
⫴	813 Light Blue
C	826 Medium Blue
⠁	948 Very Light Peach
■	800 Pale Delft Blue
P	353 Peach
◢	738 Very Light Tan
╱	745 Light Yellow
O	743 Dark Yellow
●	437 Light Tan

Backstitch Skin tone 353

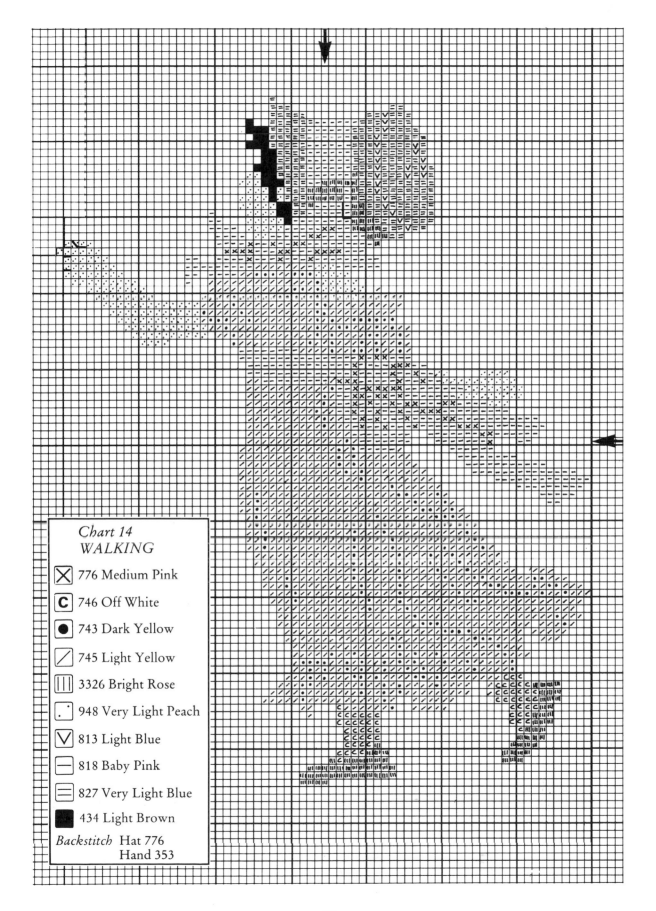

Chart 14
WALKING

☒	776 Medium Pink
C	746 Off White
●	743 Dark Yellow
╱	745 Light Yellow
⦀	3326 Bright Rose
⫶	948 Very Light Peach
V	813 Light Blue
—	818 Baby Pink
═	827 Very Light Blue
▓	434 Light Brown

Backstitch Hat 776
Hand 353

SKIPPING

WALKING

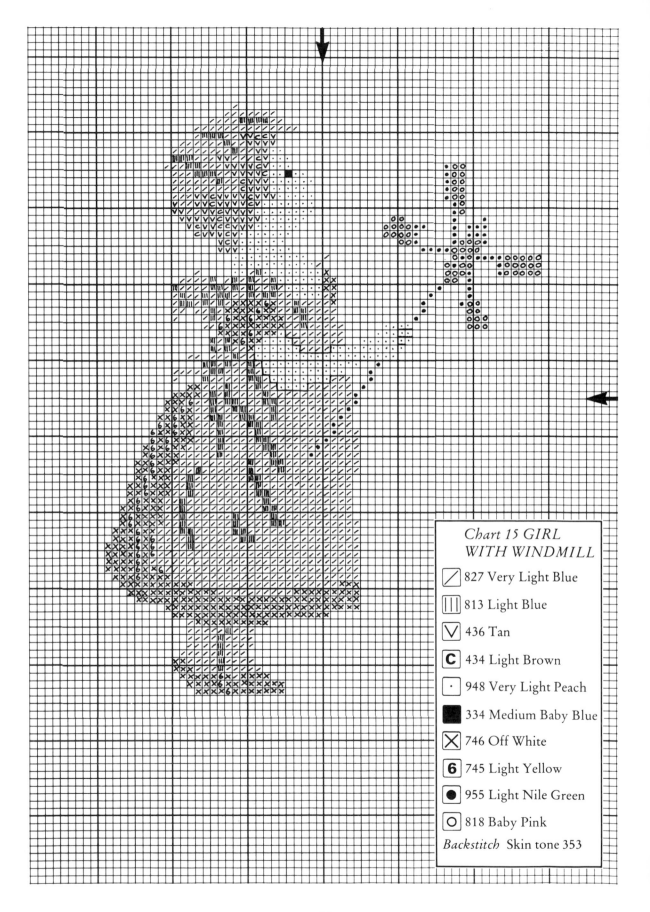

Chart 15 GIRL WITH WINDMILL

⁄	827 Very Light Blue
‖‖	813 Light Blue
V	436 Tan
C	434 Light Brown
·	948 Very Light Peach
■	334 Medium Baby Blue
X	746 Off White
6	745 Light Yellow
●	955 Light Nile Green
O	818 Baby Pink

Backstitch Skin tone 353

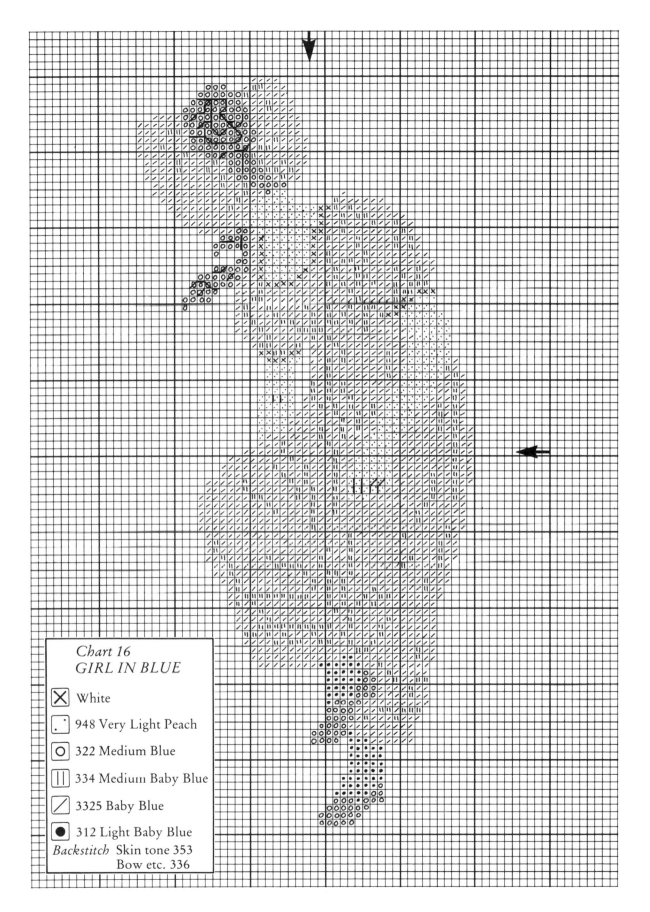

Chart 16
GIRL IN BLUE

☒ White

⚬ 948 Very Light Peach

Ⓞ 322 Medium Blue

‖ 334 Medium Baby Blue

╱ 3325 Baby Blue

● 312 Light Baby Blue

Backstitch Skin tone 353
Bow etc. 336

GIRL WITH WINDMILL

GIRL IN BLUE

FRAMED PICTURES

Girls Talk, and Dancing on the Beach
(Charts 17 & 18)

For each picture you will need:
35 x 45.5cm (13¾ x 18in) piece of ecru pearl Aida with 11 stitches to the inch.
30 x 40.5cm (11¾ x 16in) piece of mounting board
Masking tape
DMC 6-strand stranded cotton

Complete the cross-stitch embroidery using three strands of
stranded cotton.

Little Tom Tucker
(Chart 20)

30.5 x 30.5cm (12 x 12in) piece of ecru Ainring with 18 stitches to the inch.
25.5 x 25.5cm (10 x 10in) piece of mounting board
Masking tape
DMC 6-strand stranded cotton

Complete the cross-stitch embroidery using two strands of
stranded cotton.

Little Bo-Peep
(Chart 21)

33.5 x 39.5cm (13¼ x 15½in) piece of sky-blue Ainring with 18 stitches to the inch.
28.5 x 34.5cm (11¼ x 13½in) piece of mounting board
Masking tape
DMC 6-strand stranded cotton

Complete the cross-stitch embroidery using two strands of
stranded cotton.

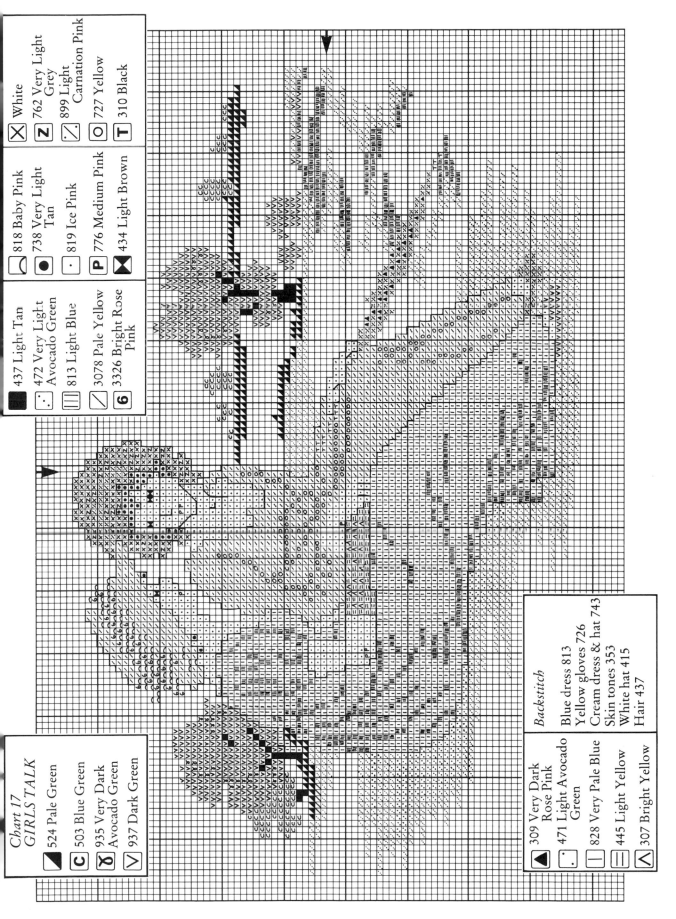

Chart 17
GIRLS TALK

◣	524 Pale Green
C	503 Blue Green
⊗	935 Very Dark Avocado Green
V	937 Dark Green

⊠	White
Z	762 Very Light Grey
⸝	899 Light Carnation Pink
O	727 Yellow
T	310 Black

◗	818 Baby Pink
●	738 Very Light Tan
·	819 Ice Pink
P	776 Medium Pink
⊠	434 Light Brown

■	437 Light Tan
∴	472 Very Light Avocado Green
‖	813 Light Blue
/	3078 Pale Yellow
6	3326 Bright Rose Pink

◀	309 Very Dark Rose Pink
∴	471 Light Avocado Green
‖	828 Very Pale Blue
≡	445 Light Yellow
∧	307 Bright Yellow

Backstitch

Blue dress 813
Yellow gloves 726
Cream dress & hat 743
Skin tones 353
White hat 415
Hair 437

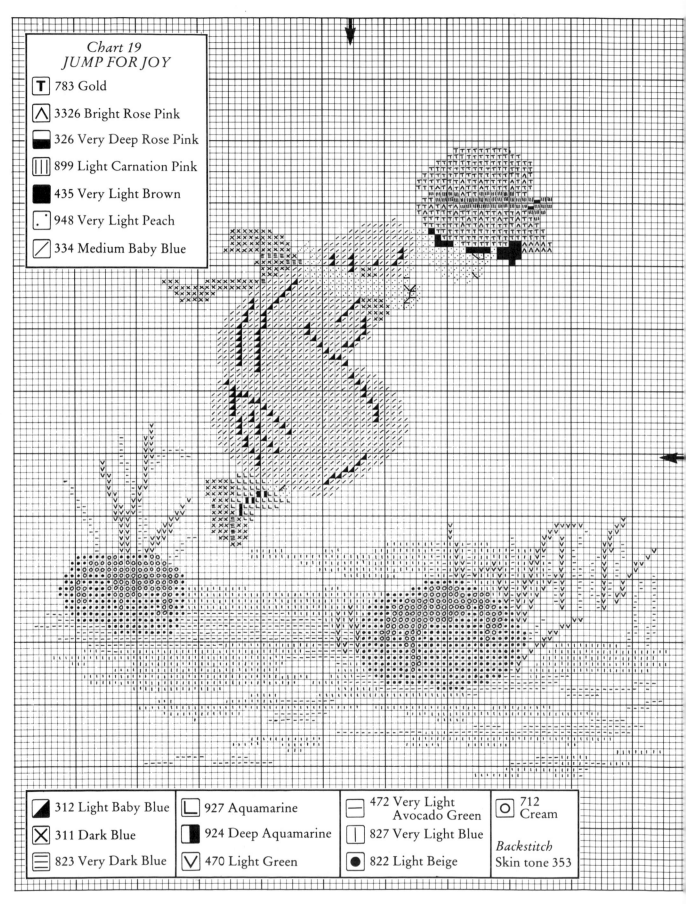

Chart 19
JUMP FOR JOY

T	783 Gold
Λ	3326 Bright Rose Pink
▬	326 Very Deep Rose Pink
⫼	899 Light Carnation Pink
■	435 Very Light Brown
·	948 Very Light Peach
╱	334 Medium Baby Blue

◢	312 Light Baby Blue
⊠	311 Dark Blue
⊟	823 Very Dark Blue
L	927 Aquamarine
▌	924 Deep Aquamarine
V	470 Light Green
⊟	472 Very Light Avocado Green
⏐	827 Very Light Blue
●	822 Light Beige
⊙	712 Cream

Backstitch
Skin tone 353

Jump for Joy
(Chart 19)

37 x 39.5cm (14½ x 15½in) piece of white Linda with 27 stitches to the inch.
32 x 34.5cm (12½ x 13½in) piece of mounting board
Masking tape
DMC 6-strand stranded cotton

Complete the cross-stitch embroidery using three strands of stranded cotton, sewing across two squares of the Linda, effectively making it fourteen to the inch.

Polly Flinders and Friends, and Polly and Friends Dancing
(Charts 22 & 23)

For each picture you will need:
41.5 x 47cm (16½ x 18½in) piece of cream fine Aida with 14 stitches to the inch.
36.5 x 42cm (14½ x 16½in) piece of mounting board.
Masking tape
DMC 6-strand stranded cotton.

Complete the cross-stitch embroidery using two strands of stranded cotton.

These projects have more backstitch than the other pictures.
The backstitch colours are shown on the key, alongside their associated main colours.

MOUNTING

When you have completed your cross-stitch embroidery, press it so that it is nice and flat, ready for mounting. Mount your embroidery by stretching it over the mounting board. To do this, place the embroidery face down on to a clean flat surface and place the mounting board centrally on to it. Fold one edge of the fabric over the mounting board (making sure it is perfectly straight) and secure with pins along the edge of the board. Secure the opposite edge in the same way, ensuring that the fabric is straight and taut on the board. Use masking tape to secure the fabric on the back of the mounting board and remove the pins. Repeat this procedure on the remaining two edges.

Your embroidery picture is now ready to be framed. The best result will be achieved if you take it to a professional framer.

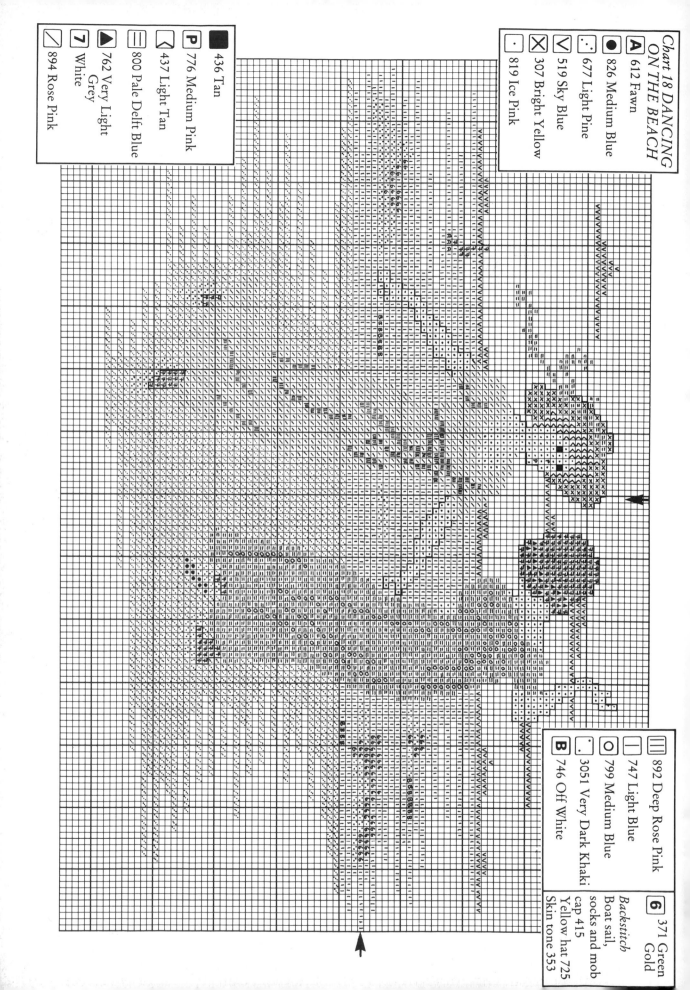

Chart 18 DANCING ON THE BEACH

A	612 Fawn
●	826 Medium Blue
∴	677 Light Pine
∨	519 Sky Blue
X	307 Bright Yellow
·	819 Ice Pink

‖‖	892 Deep Rose Pink
l	747 Light Blue
O	799 Medium Blue
·	3051 Very Dark Khaki
B	746 Off White

6	371 Green Gold

Backstitch
Boat sail,
socks and mob
cap 415
Yellow hat 725
Skin tone 353

■	436 Tan
P	776 Medium Pink
∖	437 Light Tan
≡	800 Pale Delft Blue
▲	762 Very Light Grey
7	White
∕	894 Rose Pink

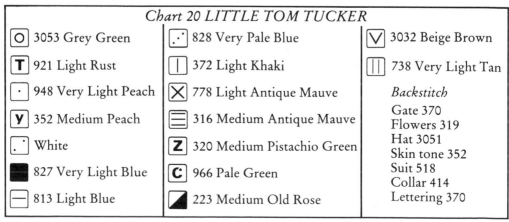

Chart 20 LITTLE TOM TUCKER

O	3053 Grey Green	∴ 828 Very Pale Blue	V 3032 Beige Brown
T	921 Light Rust		372 Light Khaki	||| 738 Very Light Tan
·	948 Very Light Peach	X 778 Light Antique Mauve	*Backstitch*
Y	352 Medium Peach	≡ 316 Medium Antique Mauve	Gate 370
·	White	Z 320 Medium Pistachio Green	Flowers 319
	827 Very Light Blue	C 966 Pale Green	Hat 3051
—	813 Light Blue	◢ 223 Medium Old Rose	Skin tone 352

Backstitch
Gate 370
Flowers 319
Hat 3051
Skin tone 352
Suit 518
Collar 414
Lettering 370

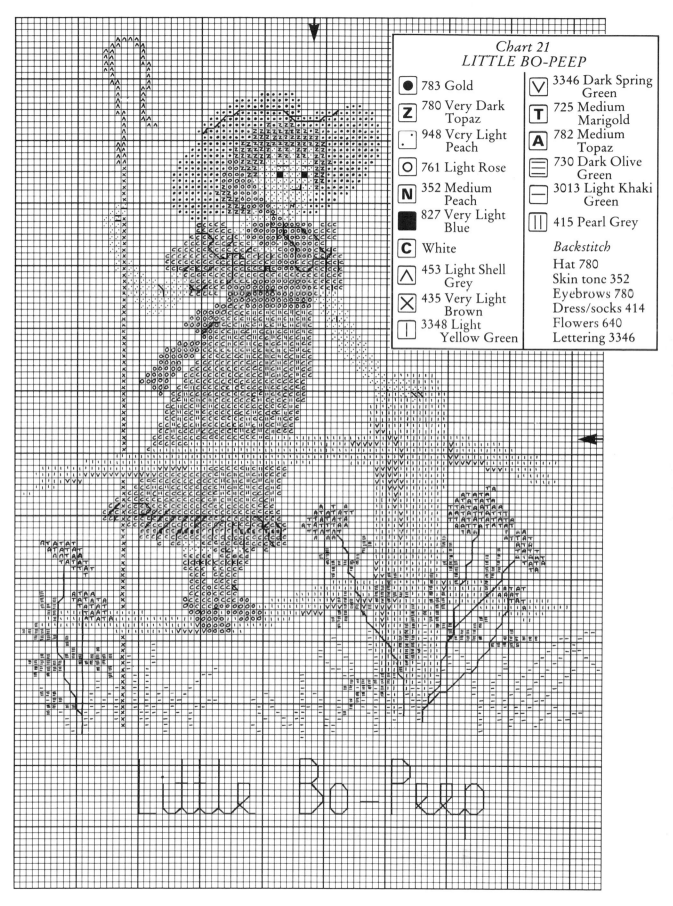

Chart 21
LITTLE BO-PEEP

- ● 783 Gold
- **Z** 780 Very Dark Topaz
- ⊡ 948 Very Light Peach
- **O** 761 Light Rose
- **N** 352 Medium Peach
- ■ 827 Very Light Blue
- **C** White
- ∧ 453 Light Shell Grey
- ✗ 435 Very Light Brown
- **I** 3348 Light Yellow Green
- **V** 3346 Dark Spring Green
- **T** 725 Medium Marigold
- **A** 782 Medium Topaz
- ≡ 730 Dark Olive Green
- − 3013 Light Khaki Green
- ‖ 415 Pearl Grey

Backstitch
Hat 780
Skin tone 352
Eyebrows 780
Dress/socks 414
Flowers 640
Lettering 3346

Little Tom Tucker

Little Bo-Peep

Chart 22
POLLY FLINDERS
AND FRIENDS

931 Medium Antique Blue
(*Backstitch* 336)

827 Very Light Blue
(*Backstitch* 336)

Very Light Peach
(*Backstitch* 351)

353 Peach

869 Warm Brown

422 Light Biscuit
(*Backstitch* 898)

White

822 Light Beige Grey

644 Medium Beige Grey
(*Backstitch* 640)

677 Light Pine

3046 Medium Yellow Beige
(*Backstitch* 680, eyebrows & hair)

352 Medium Peach

351 Coral

648 Light Beaver Grey

646 Grey (backstitch 844)

645 Dark Pewter Grey

3024 Very Light Brown Grey

3023 Light Brown Grey

3022 Medium Brown Grey

950 Medium Flesh

407 Light Brown

758 Light Dusty Rose

356 Melon Pink (*Backstitch* 355)

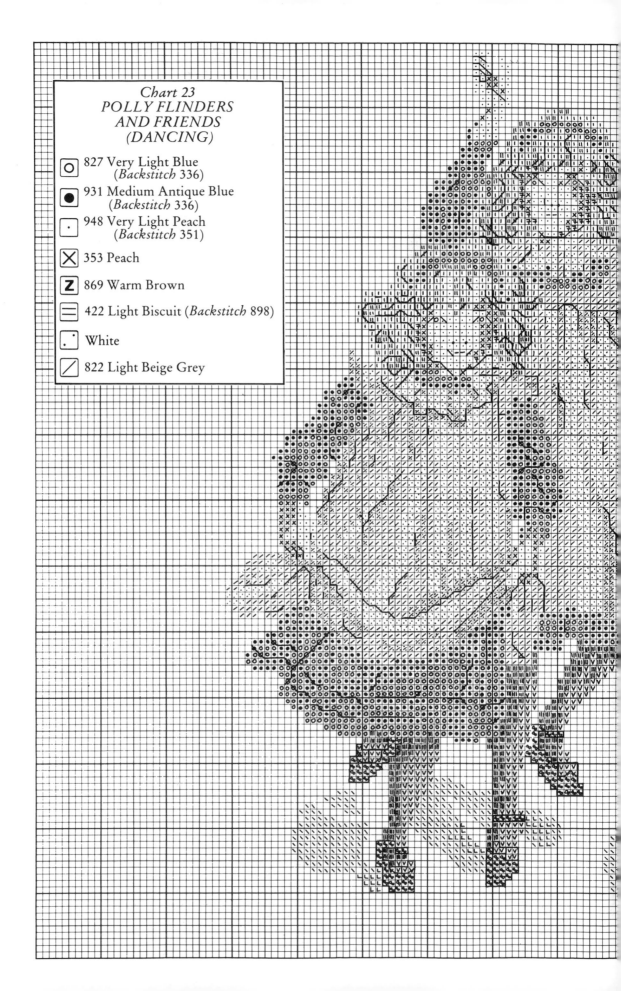

Chart 23
POLLY FLINDERS
AND FRIENDS
(DANCING)

⊙ 827 Very Light Blue
  (*Backstitch* 336)

● 931 Medium Antique Blue
  (*Backstitch* 336)

· 948 Very Light Peach
  (*Backstitch* 351)

✕ 353 Peach

Z 869 Warm Brown

≡ 422 Light Biscuit (*Backstitch* 898)

· White

╱ 822 Light Beige Grey

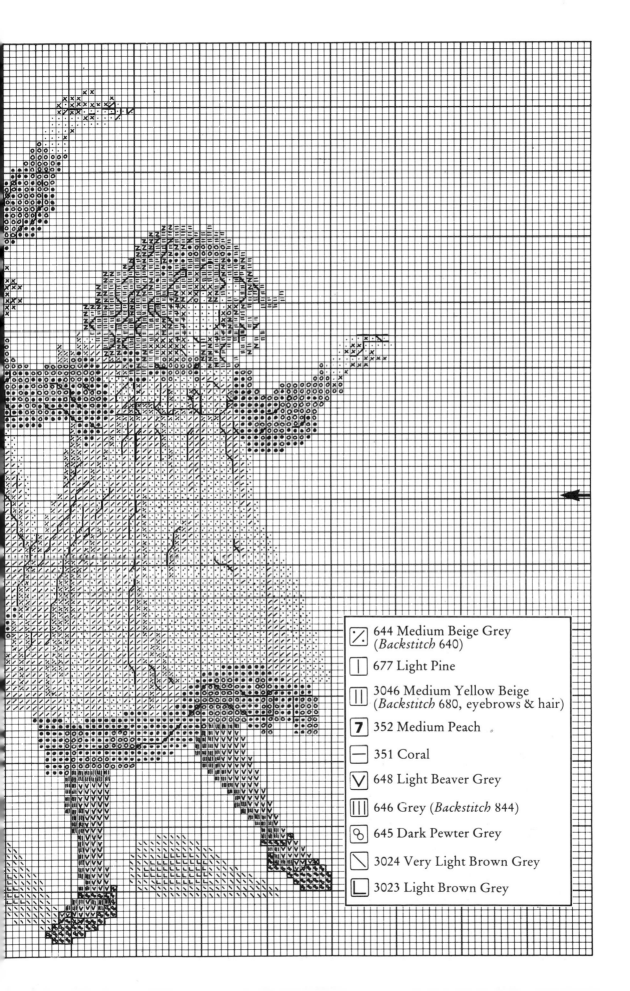

644 Medium Beige Grey
(*Backstitch* 640)

677 Light Pine

3046 Medium Yellow Beige
(*Backstitch* 680, eyebrows & hair)

7 352 Medium Peach

351 Coral

V 648 Light Beaver Grey

646 Grey (*Backstitch* 844)

645 Dark Pewter Grey

3024 Very Light Brown Grey

3023 Light Brown Grey

LAVENDER BAGS

A dainty lace-trimmed lavender bag is far too pretty to be hidden away inside your wardrobe. Try hanging it on a handle or even on the bed-post to make your bedroom smell fragrant. This pensive pair is sewn on a sky-blue background for an unusual and striking effect. (Charts 24 & 25)

MATERIALS
For each bag you will need:
17 x 17cm (6¾ x 6¾in) square of sky-blue Ainring with 18 stitches per inch
17 x 17cm (6¾ x 6¾in) square of sky-blue fabric for the backing
(These measurements include a 12mm (½in) seam allowance)
50cm (19¾in) white ribbon 6mm (¼in) wide
70cm (27½in) white lace 2cm (1in) wide
Small bag of kapok
Small amount of lavender
Adhesive
DMC 6-strand stranded cotton
Sewing thread to match the fabric

DIRECTIONS
Complete your cross-stitch embroidery centrally on the Ainring using two strands of stranded cotton. When completed, press flat.

Making up the bag

1 Pin the ribbon and lace on to the Ainring just over the stitching line and tack.

2 Place the backing material on to the Ainring, right sides together. Pin and tack.

3 Either machine- or hand-stitch together, leaving an opening on one side of about 4cm (1½in) for turning.

4 Remove the pins and tacking stitches and turn to the right side.

5 Use a scrap piece of backing material to make a lavender sachet. Place this inside the bag and fix it to the wrong side of the Ainring using a small amount of adhesive.

6 Fill the bag with kapok, using small amounts at a time to get an even filling.
Hand-stitch the opening closed.

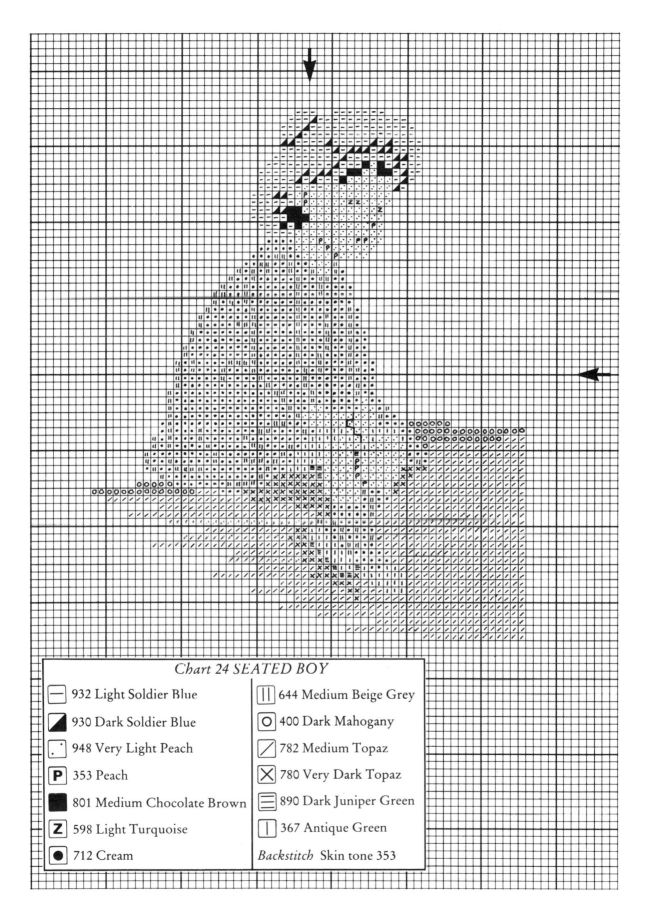

Chart 24 SEATED BOY

— 932 Light Soldier Blue	‖ 644 Medium Beige Grey
◢ 930 Dark Soldier Blue	O 400 Dark Mahogany
. 948 Very Light Peach	/ 782 Medium Topaz
P 353 Peach	X 780 Very Dark Topaz
■ 801 Medium Chocolate Brown	≡ 890 Dark Juniper Green
Z 598 Light Turquoise		367 Antique Green
● 712 Cream	*Backstitch* Skin tone 353

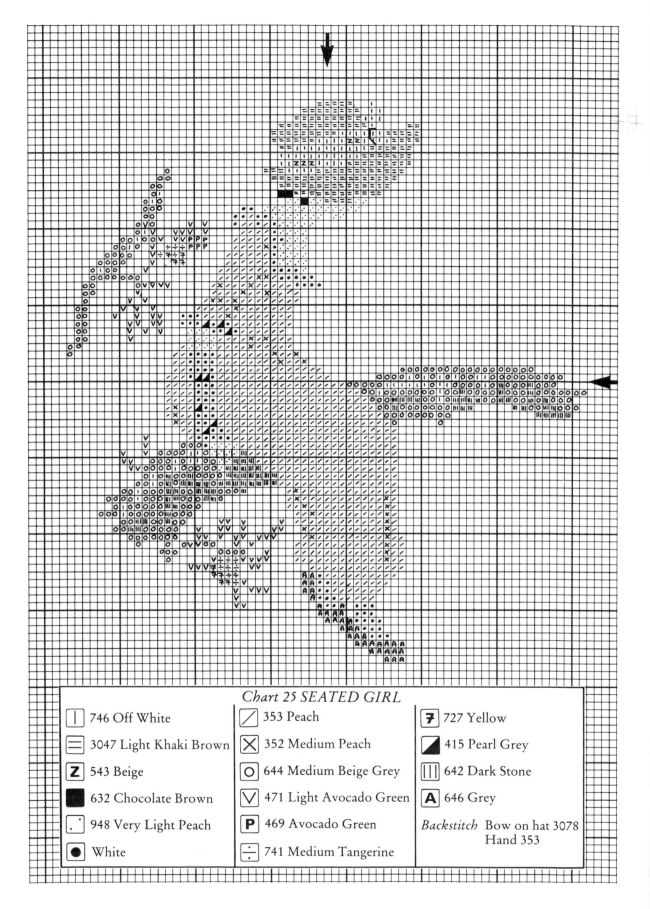

Chart 25 SEATED GIRL

	746 Off White		353 Peach		727 Yellow
	3047 Light Khaki Brown		352 Medium Peach		415 Pearl Grey
Z	543 Beige	O	644 Medium Beige Grey		642 Dark Stone
	632 Chocolate Brown	V	471 Light Avocado Green	A	646 Grey
.	948 Very Light Peach	P	469 Avocado Green		
●	White	÷	741 Medium Tangerine		

Backstitch Bow on hat 3078
Hand 353

GREETINGS CARDS

These designs are quick to sew and make a charming, personalised alternative to buying a card. A cross-stitch gift such as a paperweight or lavender bag could be combined with a cross-stitch card, for an original gift. (Chart 26)

MATERIALS
DMC special occasion cards:

Girl in White: pink card with 9 x 5cm (3½ x 2in) rectangular cut-out
Circle Design: white card with 6cm (2½in) round cut-out
Boy in Suit: blue card with 11 x 8cm (4½ x 3in) rectangular cut-out
Small Child: white card with 8 x 5cm (3 x 2in) oval cut-out
Girl in Pink: blue card with 10 x 8cm (4 x 3in) oval cut-out
Kite: white card with 10 x 5cm (3 x 2in) oval cut-out

White Hardanger with 22 stitches to the inch for all designs except the kite
Cream Hardanger with 22 stitches to the inch for the kite
DMC 6-strand stranded cotton
Double-sided adhesive tape

DIRECTIONS
To economise on fabric, cut a piece large enough to sew on several designs (remembering to space them well), rather than cutting a small piece for each design.
Complete the cross-stitch embroidery using one strand of stranded cotton. When you have completed the cross-stitch embroideries, centralise the design in the card 'window' and trim the fabric to fit.
Use double-sided tape to fix the design into the card and press the backing down firmly (see the diagram).

Fig 7 MAKING UP THE GREETINGS CARDS

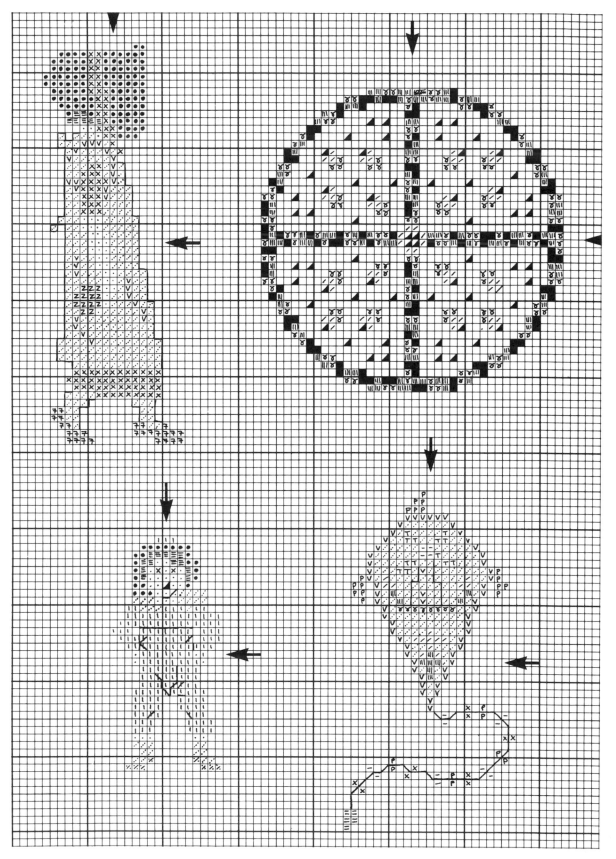

Chart 26a GIRL IN WHITE, CIRCLE DESIGN, SMALL CHILD, KITE

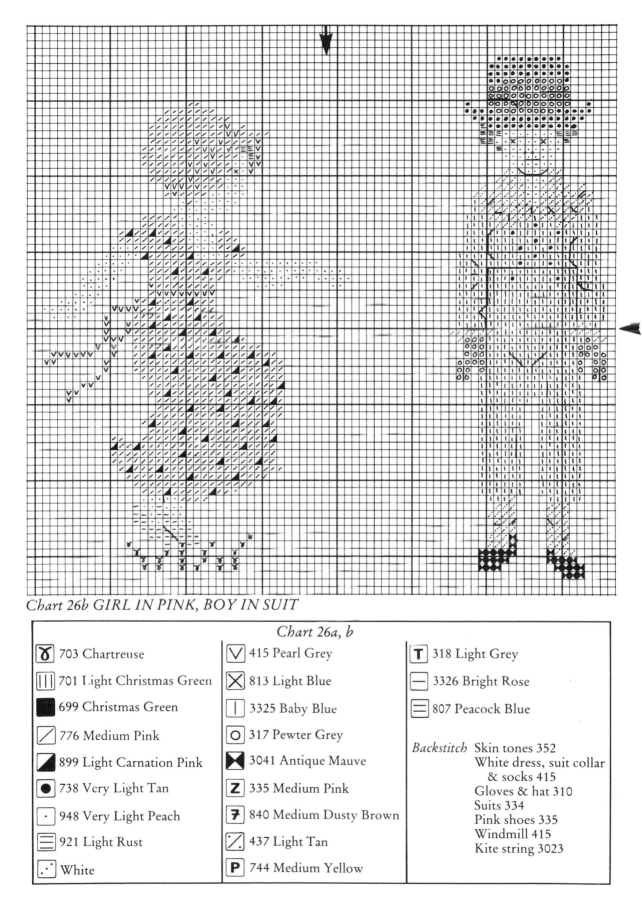

Chart 26b GIRL IN PINK, BOY IN SUIT

Chart 26a, b

ϒ 703 Chartreuse	V 415 Pearl Grey	T 318 Light Grey
||| 701 Light Christmas Green	X 813 Light Blue	— 3326 Bright Rose
■ 699 Christmas Green	I 3325 Baby Blue	≡ 807 Peacock Blue
╱ 776 Medium Pink	O 317 Pewter Grey	
◣ 899 Light Carnation Pink	◪ 3041 Antique Mauve	*Backstitch* Skin tones 352
● 738 Very Light Tan	Z 335 Medium Pink	White dress, suit collar
· 948 Very Light Peach	7 840 Medium Dusty Brown	& socks 415
≡ 921 Light Rust	╱ 437 Light Tan	Gloves & hat 310
·· White	P 744 Medium Yellow	Suits 334

Backstitch Skin tones 352
White dress, suit collar
  & socks 415
Gloves & hat 310
Suits 334
Pink shoes 335
Windmill 415
Kite string 3023

MINIATURES

These delightful miniature pictures will make an attractive addition to your home, whether they are displayed singly or together. Any one of the five designs would make a lovely present. (Charts 27 & 28)

MATERIALS
DMC miniature frames as follows:

Boy and Girl, Girl Seated: 15cm (6in) round in brass
Windmill: 8cm (3in) round in brass
Two Boys: 10cm (4in) round in brass
Small Boy: 6 x 9cm (2½ x 3½in) oval in brass

Fine Aida with 14 stitches per inch (the colours chosen were cream, sage and lemon)
DMC 6-strand stranded cotton

DIRECTIONS
Use two strands of the stranded cotton to sew up your designs. When you have completed the cross-stitch embroideries, gently remove all parts of the frame and use the template provided to draw around your design, ensuring that it is central.

Next, place the clear acetate into the frame, followed by your embroidery, then the thin card followed by the backing.

Your frame is now complete.

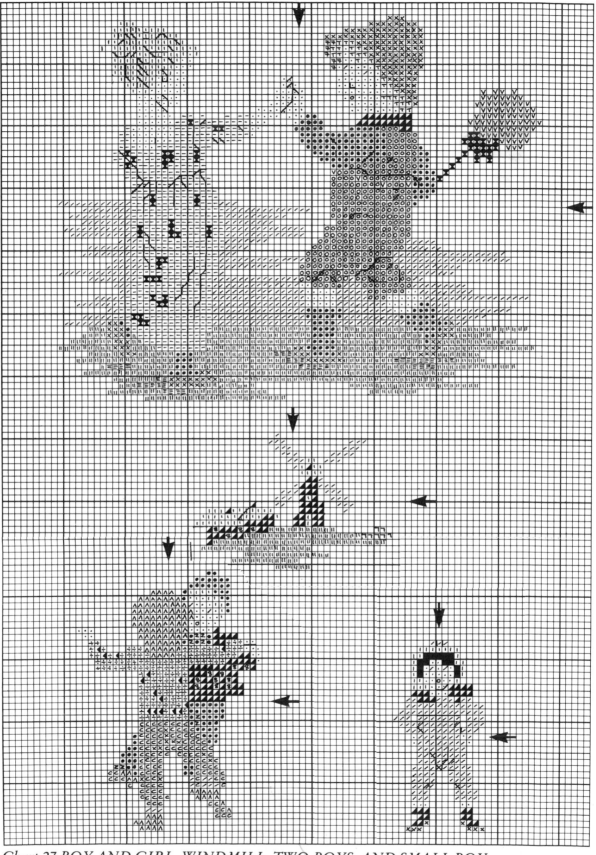

Chart 27 BOY AND GIRL, WINDMILL, TWO BOYS, AND SMALL BOY

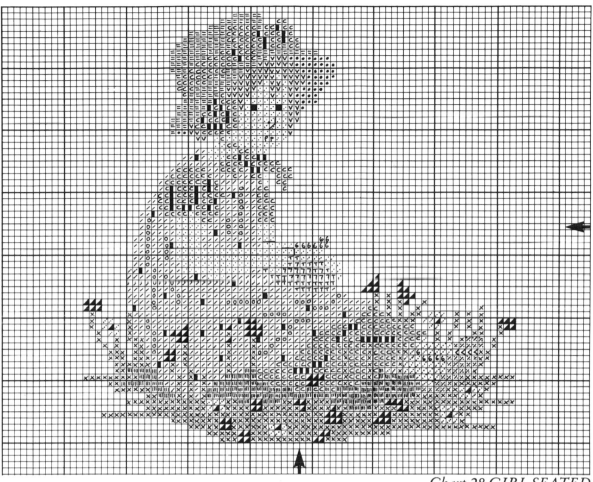

Chart 28 GIRL SEATED

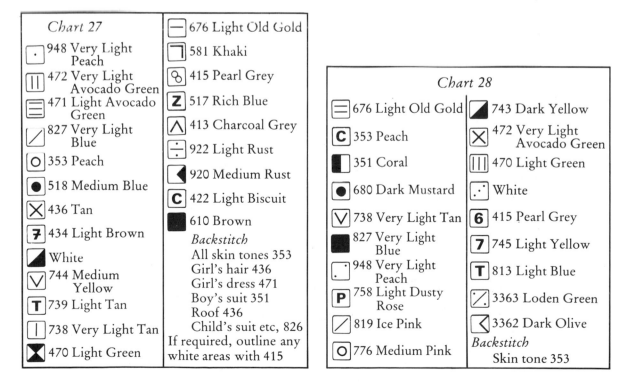

Chart 27	
⊡ 948 Very Light Peach	⊟ 676 Light Old Gold
Ⅲ 472 Very Light Avocado Green	� Ⅶ 581 Khaki
⊜ 471 Light Avocado Green	⊗ 415 Pearl Grey
⊘ 827 Very Light Blue	Ｚ 517 Rich Blue
Ｏ 353 Peach	⋀ 413 Charcoal Grey
● 518 Medium Blue	÷ 922 Light Rust
✕ 436 Tan	◀ 920 Medium Rust
７ 434 Light Brown	Ｃ 422 Light Biscuit
◢ White	■ 610 Brown
Ⅴ 744 Medium Yellow	*Backstitch*
Ｔ 739 Light Tan	All skin tones 353
Ｉ 738 Very Light Tan	Girl's hair 436
⊠ 470 Light Green	Girl's dress 471
	Boy's suit 351
	Roof 436
	Child's suit etc, 826
	If required, outline any white areas with 415

Chart 28	
⊟ 676 Light Old Gold	◤ 743 Dark Yellow
Ｃ 353 Peach	✕ 472 Very Light Avocado Green
▮ 351 Coral	Ⅲ 470 Light Green
● 680 Dark Mustard	⠒ White
Ⅴ 738 Very Light Tan	6 415 Pearl Grey
■ 827 Very Light Blue	７ 745 Light Yellow
⠒ 948 Very Light Peach	Ｔ 813 Light Blue
Ｐ 758 Light Dusty Rose	⁄ 3363 Loden Green
⁄ 819 Ice Pink	◀ 3362 Dark Olive
Ｏ 776 Medium Pink	*Backstitch* Skin tone 353

89

TABLECLOTH

A tablecloth is a good way of displaying your cross-stitch expertise, and always makes a welcome gift. Used at home, this lovely tablecloth will be admired by everyone for its delicate Kate Greenaway motifs. (Charts 29 & 30)

MATERIALS

1m (39½in) cream Hardida
DMC 6-stranded cotton
Sewing thread to match the fabric

DIRECTIONS

The tablecloth is worked on Hardida which is a checkerboard fabric consisting of 8cm (3¼in) squares, alternating between Aida and Hardanger.

The finished cloth measures 94 x 94cm (37 x 37in), so you will need to cut your fabric to measure 98 x 98cm (38½ x 38½in) to allow for hemming. When you cut the fabric, ensure that you begin and end with a Hardanger square.

Begin the cross-stitch embroidery on the second row of squares using one strand of the stranded cotton. Arrange the design so that all four sides of the cloth are the same, placing the circle motif p96 (not the garland) in the centre square (see the diagram as a guide to positioning the motifs).

When you have completed the embroideries, mitre the corners of the tablecloth and hem them all around.

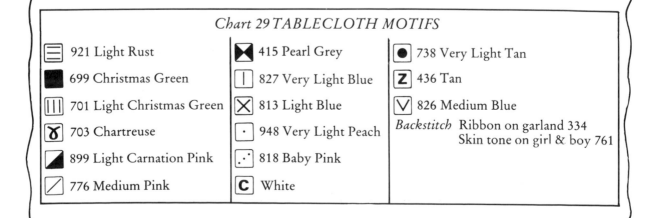

Chart 29 TABLECLOTH MOTIFS

921 Light Rust
699 Christmas Green
701 Light Christmas Green
703 Chartreuse
899 Light Carnation Pink
776 Medium Pink

415 Pearl Grey
827 Very Light Blue
813 Light Blue
948 Very Light Peach
818 Baby Pink
C White

738 Very Light Tan
Z 436 Tan
V 826 Medium Blue

Backstitch Ribbon on garland 334
Skin tone on girl & boy 761

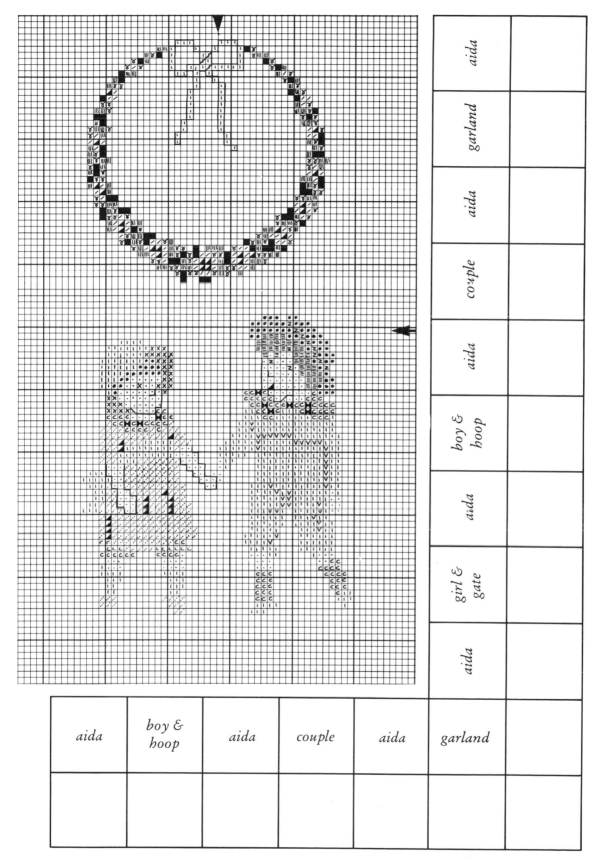

	aida	
	garland	
	aida	
	couple	
	aida	
	boy & hoop	
	aida	
	girl & gate	
	aida	

aida	boy & hoop	aida	couple	aida	garland	

POSITIONING THE MOTIFS ON THE TABLECLOTH

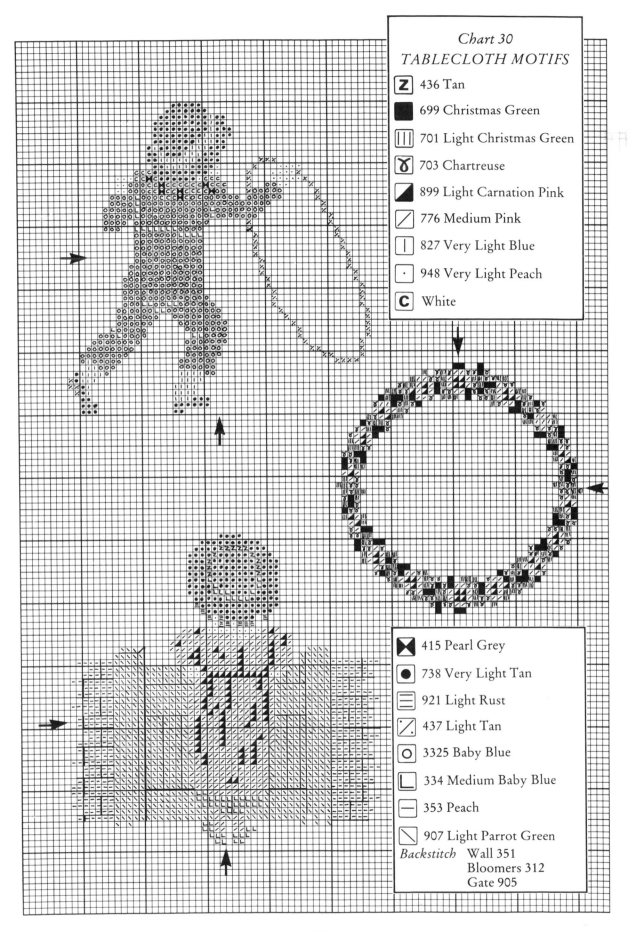

Chart 30
TABLECLOTH MOTIFS

Z	436 Tan
■	699 Christmas Green
|||	701 Light Christmas Green
ᛪ	703 Chartreuse
◤	899 Light Carnation Pink
╱	776 Medium Pink
		827 Very Light Blue
·	948 Very Light Peach
C	White

⊠	415 Pearl Grey
●	738 Very Light Tan
☰	921 Light Rust
╱	437 Light Tan
O	3325 Baby Blue
L	334 Medium Baby Blue
—	353 Peach
╲	907 Light Parrot Green

Backstitch Wall 351
Bloomers 312
Gate 905

JAM-POT COVERS

Use these easily made pretty covers to brighten up your breakfast- or tea-table. (Chart 31)

MATERIALS
White Linda with 27 stitches to the inch
Suitable fabric for backing (cotton, gingham, etc)
Narrow white lace for edging
White ribbon 6mm (¼in) wide
DMC 6-strand stranded cotton
White sewing cotton

DIRECTIONS
Complete the cross-stitch embroideries using two strands of the stranded cotton, sewing across two squares of the Linda, effectively making it 14 to the inch.

1 Measure the diameter of your jam-pot lid and add 6cm (2¼in) for seam allowances.

2 Cut a paper template circle to this diameter.

3 Ensure that the cross-stitch design is centralised, place the template over and cut out circles.

4 Cut circles of backing fabric to the same size.

5 Place right sides together and stitch 6mm (¼in) seam around the outer edge, leaving 19mm (¾in) opening.

6 Trim the seams and turn to the right side. Press flat.

7 Stitch a top seam all round 12mm (½in) from the outer edge.

8 Stitch narrow lace to the outer edge, making sure that you do not close the opening.

9 Thread the ribbon through this hem.

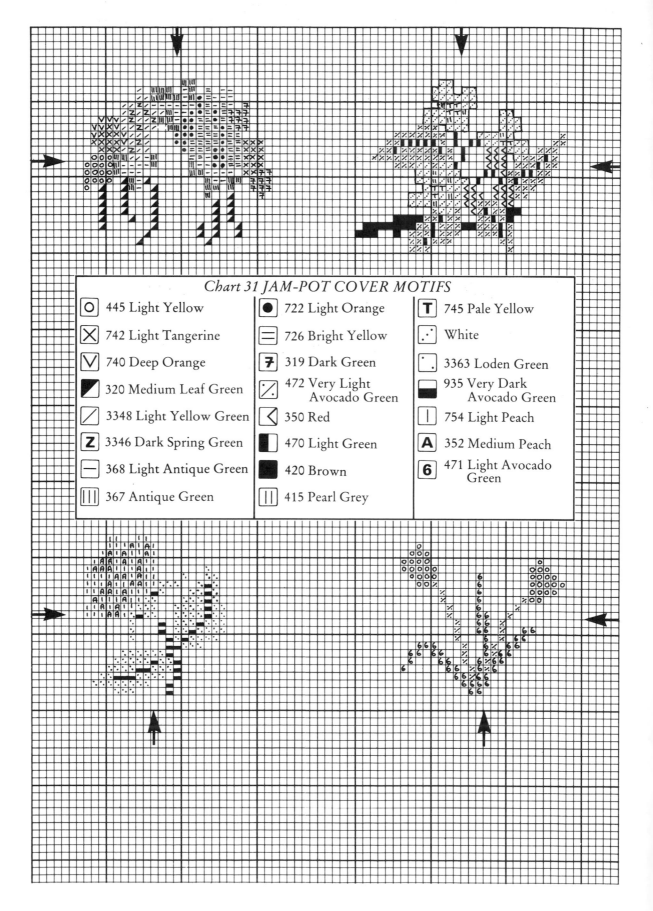

Chart 31 JAM-POT COVER MOTIFS

O	445 Light Yellow
X	742 Light Tangerine
V	740 Deep Orange
◣	320 Medium Leaf Green
╱	3348 Light Yellow Green
Z	3346 Dark Spring Green
—	368 Light Antique Green
⦀	367 Antique Green
●	722 Light Orange
=	726 Bright Yellow
7	319 Dark Green
⟋	472 Very Light Avocado Green
<	350 Red
▮	470 Light Green
■	420 Brown
‖	415 Pearl Grey
T	745 Pale Yellow
∴	White
⸪	3363 Loden Green
▬	935 Very Dark Avocado Green
I	754 Light Peach
A	352 Medium Peach
6	471 Light Avocado Green

TRINKET BOXES

Porcelain trinket boxes make beautiful gifts which are both useful and decorative. They can be used to adorn a dressing-table, small table or even a mantelpiece. A trinket box makes an ideal birthday present or even just to thank someone special. (Chart 32)

MATERIALS
DMC trinket boxes:

38mm (1½in) round porcelain trinket box in ivory (circular motif)
76mm (3in) round porcelain trinket box in pink (boy with hoop)
89 x 63mm (3½ x 2½in) oval porcelain trinket box in blue (girl in yellow)

Beige Lugana with 25 stitches per inch for circular motif
White Hardanger with 22 stitches per inch for boy and girl motifs
DMC 6-strand stranded cotton

DIRECTIONS

Complete the cross-stitch embroideries using one strand of stranded cotton.

Place the finished cross-stitch embroidery face up on a firm, flat surface. Gently remove all parts from the trinket-box lid.

Use the rim of the lid to centralise the design. When the design is centralised, draw around the outer edge on to the fabric. Remove the lid and cut the fabric to size.

To assemble the lid, replace the clear acetate and place your design centrally into the lid, with the right side to the acetate. Place the sponge behind your design. Push the metal locking disc very firmly into place using thumb pressure, with the raised side of the disc facing the sponge. When the locking disc is tightly in position, remove the protective film and, if preferred, stick the lid liner to the lid.

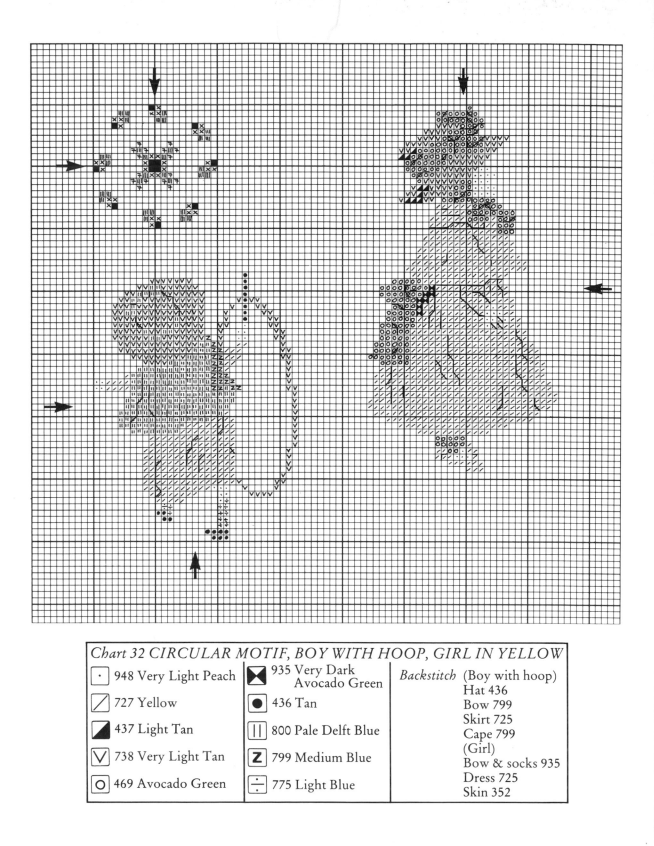

Chart 32 CIRCULAR MOTIF, BOY WITH HOOP, GIRL IN YELLOW

· 948 Very Light Peach	935 Very Dark Avocado Green	*Backstitch* (Boy with hoop) Hat 436
727 Yellow	● 436 Tan	Bow 799 Skirt 725
437 Light Tan	‖ 800 Pale Delft Blue	Cape 799 (Girl)
V 738 Very Light Tan	Z 799 Medium Blue	Bow & socks 935 Dress 725
O 469 Avocado Green	÷ 775 Light Blue	Skin 352

PAPERWEIGHTS

These pretty paperweights make an unusual gift. They can be put to practical use on a desk or be used as ornaments around the home. (Chart 33)

MATERIALS

DMC paperweights:

9cm (3½in) round paperweight (Garland)
9cm (3½in) fluted paperweight (Child Kneeling)

White Hardanger with 22 stitches per inch
DMC 6-strand stranded cotton

DIRECTIONS

Complete the embroidery using one strand of stranded cotton.
Place the completed embroidery on a firm, flat surface and use the paper template (provided with the paperweight) to draw around your design, ensuring that it is central.
Cut the fabric to size and place right side down into the recess on the base of the paperweight. Place the paper template on to the reverse side of your embroidery. Next, peel the backing off the protective base and very carefully stick it to the base of the paperweight, ensuring that the embroidery and template do not move out of place.

Chart 33 GARLAND, CHILD KNEELING	
■ 699 Christmas Green	▥ 762 Very Light Grey
▤ 701 Light Christmas Green	❘ 993 Turquoise
7 704 Medium Apple Green	⚊ 739 Light Tan
X 605 Bright Pink	⊠ 800 Pale Delft Blue
◣ 335 Medium Rose Pink	< 433 Medium Brown
V 738 Very Light Tan	*Backstitch*
· 948 Very Light Peach	Skin tone 352
O White	Socks & collar 415
	Hat 318
	Suit 991

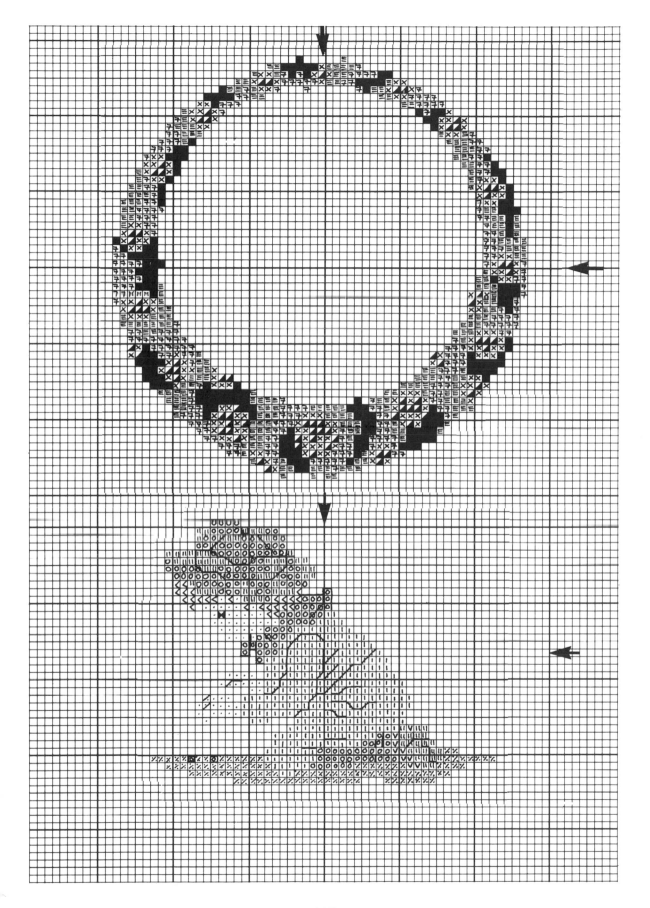

NIGHTDRESS BAG

This useful nightdress bag makes an extremely practical gift. It will be an attractive feature in the bedroom and is suitable for children of any age group. The bag has a draw-string top and is large enough to hold a child's long nightdress or a pair of pyjamas. Alternatively, it can be used as a toy- or shoe-bag. (Charts 34 & 35)

MATERIALS
2m (78¾in) baby blue ribbon 2.5cm (1in) wide
2 pieces sky-blue pearl Aida with 11 stitches to the inch,
measuring approximately 54.5 x 46cm (21½ x 18in)
2 pieces sky-blue lining fabric measuring 49.5 x 40.5cm (19½ x 16in)
DMC 6-strand stranded cotton
Pale blue sewing cotton to match fabric

DIRECTIONS
Complete the cross-stitch picture for the front of the bag using three strands of stranded cotton. Complete the poem for the back of the bag in backstitch using two strands of stranded cotton (796). Cut the pearl Aida to size 49.5 x 40.5cm (19½ x 16in) ensuring that a clearance is left around the finished embroidery of 5cm (2in) at the sides and bottom, and 14cm (5½in) at the top. These measurements include 12mm (½in) seam allowance.

MAKING UP
THE BAG

1 Place right sides together. Stitch side seams down from top for 4cm (1½in). Leave a gap of 2.5cm (1in), then recommence stitching the side seams to the bottom as shown in Fig 1. *continued on Page 112*

↕ *4cm (1½in) stitching*
↕ *2.5cm (1in) gap*

Fig 1

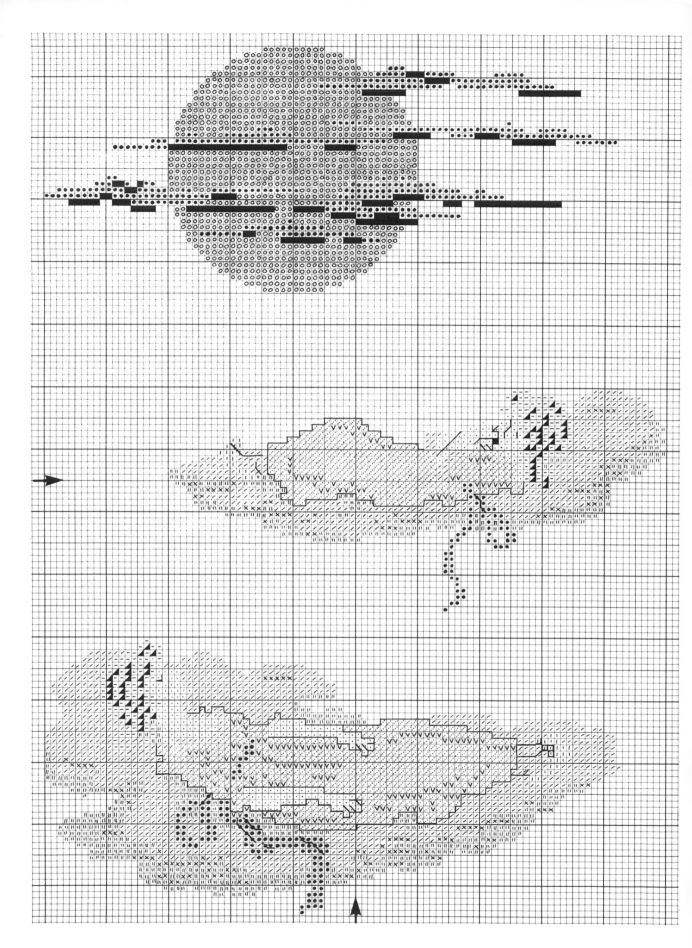

They saw it rise in the morning,
They saw it set at night,
And they longed to go and see it,
Ah! if they only might.

The little soft white clouds heard them,
And stepped from out of the blue;
And each laid a little child softly
Upon its bosom of dew.

And they carried them higher and higher,
And they nothing knew any more
Until they were standing waiting
In front of the round gold door.

And they knocked, and called, and entreated,
Whoever should be within;
But all to no purpose, for no one
Would hearken to let them in.

Chart 35 POEM FOR BACK OF NIGHTDRESS BAG

Chart 34 DESIGN FOR FRONT OF NIGHTDRESS BAG		
O 744 Medium Yellow	/ White	V 336 Dark Blue
● 754 Light Peach	— 676 Light Old Gold	I 745 Light Yellow
■ 352 Medium Peach	◣ 680 Dark Mustard	*Backstitch* Bow 352
X 415 Pearl Grey	· 948 Very Light Peach	Skin tone 352
II 762 Very Light Grey	∴ 322 Medium Blue	Shoes 743
		Arms in lower figure 353

2 Press side seams open around gap and top stitch 6mm (¼in) from the edge as shown in Fig 2.

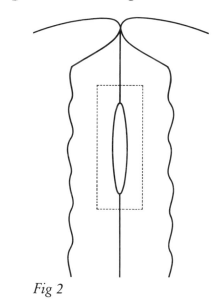

Fig 2

3 Stitch the bottom seam.

4 Turn to the right side and press. Try not to iron over the embroidery.

5 Lining: place the two pieces of lining fabric right sides together. Stitch the side seams. Stitch the bottom seam, leaving an opening of 10cm (4in) for turning inside out (see Fig 3). *Do not turn yet.*

6 Place the outer bag into the lining, right sides together. Stitch around the top edge.

7 Turn right side out, easing through the opening at the bottom of the lining. Hand-stitch lining together at the bottom.

8 Press the top edge of bag along the seam.

9 Top stitch around the bag 6mm (¼in) above the ribbon opening and again below (see Fig 4).

10 Take the ribbon and thread it twice round through the casement made by the two rows of stitches. Join the ends together.

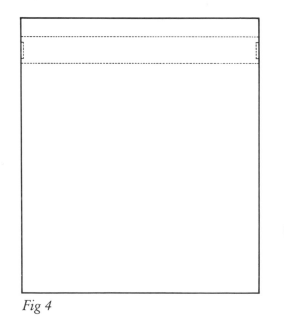

10cm
(4in)

Fig 3

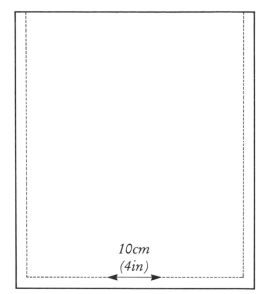

Fig 4

CHILD'S SKIRT

This pretty skirt, with its embroidered 'frieze' of Kate Greenaway girls, is designed to fit a 5- to 6-year-old child. It is very simple to make and looks lovely when complemented with a little lacy blouse. (Chart 36)

MATERIALS
50cm (19¾in) skirt fabric
50cm (19¾in) elastic 2cm (¾in) wide
1m (39½in) white Ainring with 18 stitches to the inch
DMC 6-strand stranded cotton
Sewing cotton to match fabric

DIRECTIONS
The embroidered strip for the skirt consists of three repeats of the charted design (see Fig 1).
Use one strand of stranded cotton to sew the cross-stitch designs.
Cut the finished embroidered strip (D) to size 82 x 14cm (32¼ x 5½in).
All measurements include a 12mm (½in) seam allowance on all edges.
Cut the skirt fabric as follows:
   Top strip (A): 82 x 14cm
      (32¼ x 5½in)
   Bottom strip (B): 82 x 10cm
      (32¼ x 4in)
   Waist strip (C): 82 x 8cm
      (32¼ x 3in)
Join strips together as in Fig 1.

Fig 1

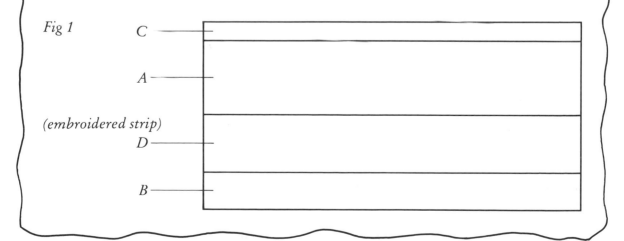

C

A

(embroidered strip)
D

B

Press the seams as follows:

Press the seam between C and A towards the top.
Press the seam between C and D towards the top.
Press the seam between D and B towards the bottom.

With wrong sides together, join the back seam leaving a 2cm (¾in) opening 1.5cm (⅝in) from the top edge (see Fig 2).

Press in a 1cm (½in) seam allowance on the top and bottom edges of the skirt.
Fold a 4cm (1½in) hem at the bottom and hand-hem in place.
Fold a 3cm (1¼in) hem on the waist strip. Top stitch with a machine 6mm (¼in) from both edges of this hem. Thread the elastic through between these two rows of stitches and join the ends together.
Your skirt is now complete.

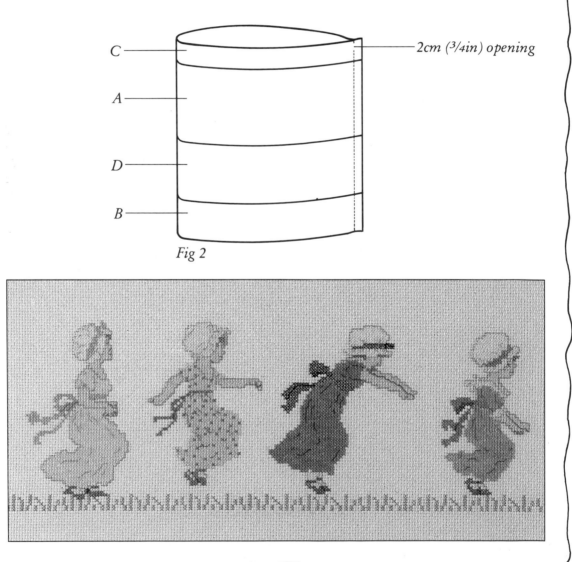

C ──────── 2cm (¾in) opening

A

D

B

Fig 2

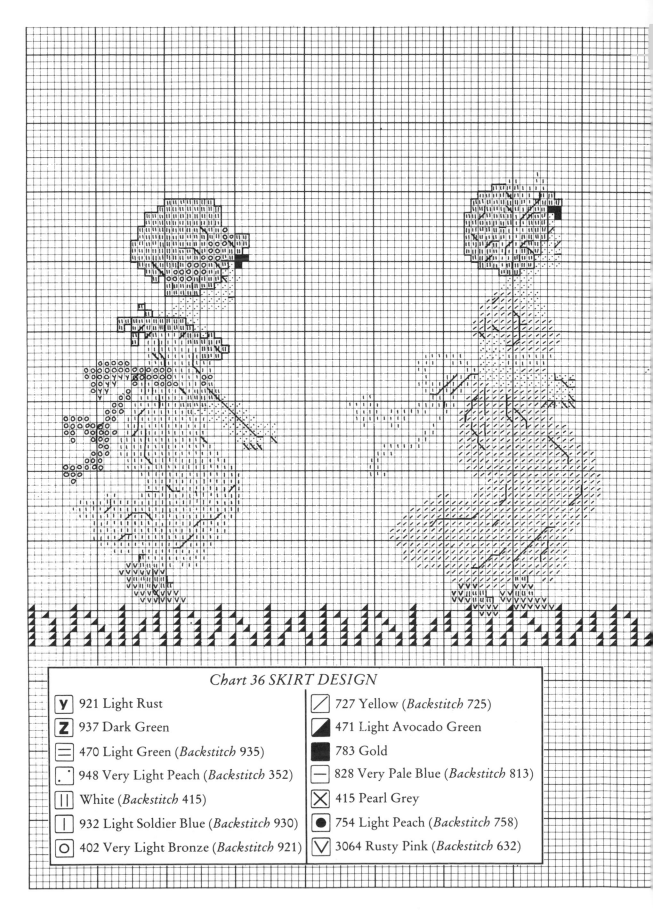

Chart 36 SKIRT DESIGN

Y	921 Light Rust	/	727 Yellow (*Backstitch 725*)
Z	937 Dark Green	◢	471 Light Avocado Green
=	470 Light Green (*Backstitch 935*)	◼	783 Gold
.	948 Very Light Peach (*Backstitch 352*)	—	828 Very Pale Blue (*Backstitch 813*)
‖	White (*Backstitch 415*)	☒	415 Pearl Grey
│	932 Light Soldier Blue (*Backstitch 930*)	●	754 Light Peach (*Backstitch 758*)
O	402 Very Light Bronze (*Backstitch 921*)	V	3064 Rusty Pink (*Backstitch 632*)

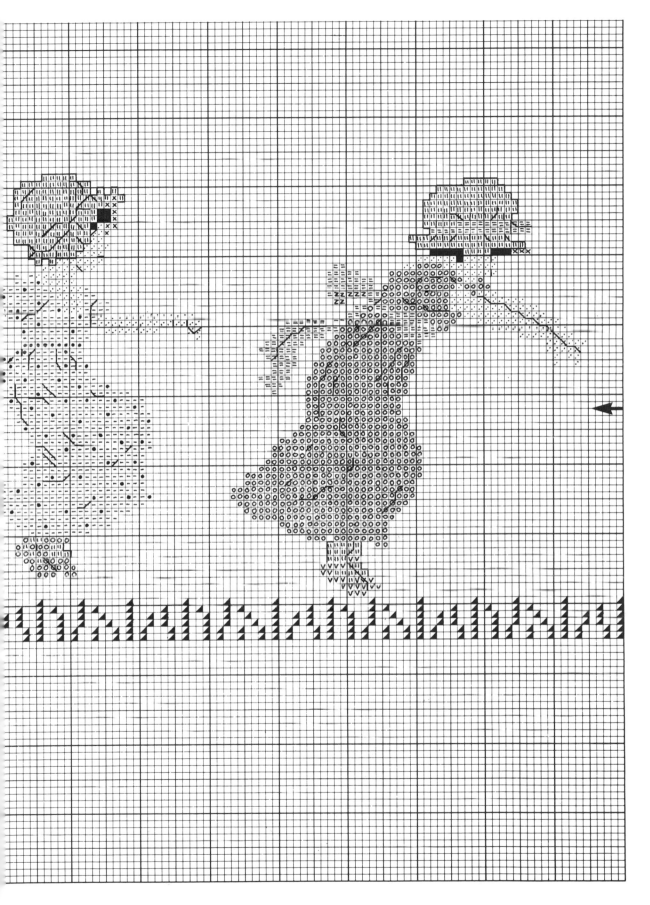

BIBLIOGRAPHY

Books illustrated and partly illustrated by Kate Greenaway.

1867 *Infant Amusements, or How to Make a Nursery Happy* by William H.G. Kingston. Frontispiece by Kate Greenaway (Griffith & Farran, London)

1870 *Aunt Louisa's Nursery Favourite: Diamonds and Toads* from a series of London Toybooks. Illustrations by Kate Greenaway (Frederick Warne & Co, London)

1871 *My School Days in Paris* by Margaret S. Jeune. Illustrations by Kate Greenaway (Griffith & Farran, London)

c.1871 Madame d'Aulnoy's fairy tales:
The Fair One with Golden Locks
The Babes in the Wood
Tom Thumb
Bluebeard
Puss in Boots
The Blue Bird
The White Cat
Hop o' My Thumb
Red Riding Hood

Issued separately and illustrated by Kate Greenaway (Gall & Inglis, Edinburgh)

1874 *The Children of the Parsonage* by Aunt Cae. Illustrations by Kate Greenaway (Griffith & Farran, London; second edition issued in 1875)

1875 *Fairy Gifts; or A Wallet of Wonders* by Kathleen Knox. Illustrations and woodcuts by Kate Greenaway, engraved by John Greenaway. (Griffith & Farran, London; E.P. Dutton & Co, New York; reissued in 1882 and 1884)
The Fairy Spinner by Miranda Hill. Illustrations by Kate Greenaway (Marcus Ward & Co, London)
A Cruise in the Acorn by Alice Jerrold. Illustrations by Kate Greenaway; also issued as greeting cards (Marcus Ward & Co, London)
A Calendar of the Seasons for 1876. Illustrations by Kate Greenaway; the illustrations were later used in *Flowers and Fancies*, 1883 (Marcus Ward & Co, London)
Turnaside Cottage by Mary Senior Clark. Illustrations by Kate Greenaway (Marcus Ward & Co, London)

c.1875 *Melcomb Manor: A Family Chronicle* by Frederick Scarlett Potter. Illustrations by Kate Greenaway (Marcus Ward & Co, London)
Children's Songs (Marcus Ward & Co, London)

1876 *A Calendar of the Seasons for 1877.* Illustrations by Kate Greenaway (Marcus Ward & Co, London)

1877 *Tom Seven Years Old* by H. Rutherford Russell. Illustrations by Kate Greenaway (Marcus Ward & Co, London)

The Quiver of Love: A Collection of Valentines Ancient and Modern. Illustrations by Walter Crane and Kate Greenaway (Marcus Ward and Co, London)
Seven Birthdays or The Children of Fortune, A Fairy Chronicle by Kathleen Knox. Illustrations by Kate Greenaway (Griffith & Farran, London)
Starlight Stories Told to Bright Eyes and Listening Ears by Fanny Lablache. Illustrations by Kate Greenaway (Griffith & Farran, London)

1878 *Poor Nelly* by Mrs Bonavia Hunt. Illustrations by Kate Greenaway; the story was serialised in *Little Folks* in 1877 (Cassell, Petter, Gilpin, London)
Topo: A Tale About English Children in Italy by G.E. Brunefille. Illustrations by Kate Greenaway (Marcus Ward & Co. London; second edition, 1880)

Under the Window by Kate Greenaway, engraved and printed by Edmund Evans (George Routledge, London)

1879 *The Heir of Redclyffe* by Charlotte M. Yonge. Illustrations by Kate Greenaway (Macmillan & Co, London; another edition, 1901)
Heartsease; or The Brother's Wife by Charlotte M. Yonge. Illustrations by Kate Greenaway; another edition, 1901 (Macmillan & Co, London)
Amateur Theatricals by Walter Herries Pollock. Illustrations by Kate Greenaway (Macmillan & Co, London)
Trot's Journey by Kate Greenaway (R. Worthington, New York; originally published in *Little Folks* in January 1879)
Toyland, Trot's Journey, and Other Poems and Stories. Illustrations by Kate Greenaway (R. Worthington, New York)
The 'Little Folks' Painting Book. Engravings by Kate Greenaway and verses and stories by George Weatherly (Cassell, Petter, Gilpin, London)

c.1879 *The 'Little Folks' Nature Painting Book.* Illustrations by Kate Greenaway with stories and verses by George Weatherly (Cassell, Petter, Gilpin, London)
A Favourite Album of Fun and Fancy with illustrations by Kate Greenaway to the allegory of 'Kribs and the Wonderful Bird' (Cassell, Petter, Gilpin, London)
Three Brown Boys and Other Happy Children by Ellen Haile. Illustrations by Kate Greenaway and others (Cassell & Co, New York)
The Two Gray Girls and Their Opposite Neighbours by Ellen Haile. Illustrations by Kate Greenaway, M.E. Edwards and others. (Cassell & Co, New York)

1880 *Kate Greenaway's Birthday Book for Children.* Illustrations by Kate Greenaway, printed by Edmund Evans (George Routledge, London)
Freddie's Letter: Stories for Little People. Frontispiece by Kate Greenaway (George Routledge, London)

Calendar of the Seasons for 1881. Illustrations by Kate Greenaway (Marcus Ward & Co, London)

c.1880 *The Old Farm Gate.* Illustrations by Kate Greenaway, M.E. Edwards and Miriam Kerns (George Routledge, London)

1881 *The Library* by Andrew Lang. Austin Dobson wrote a chapter on modern English illustrated books, including illustrations by Kate Greenaway (Macmillan & Co, London)
London Lyrics by Frederick Locker. Tailpiece by Kate Greenaway (White Stokes & Allen, London; American edition, 1886, New York)
A Day in a Child's Life with music by Myles Foster. Illustrations by Kate Greenaway, engraved and printed by Edmund Evans (George Routledge, London)
Mother Goose or The Old Nursery Rhymes. Illustrations by Kate Greenaway, engraved and printed by Edmund Evans (George Routledge, London)

1882 *The Illustrated Children's Birthday Book* written in part and edited by F.E. Weatherly. Illustrations by Kate Greenaway and others (W. Mack, London)

1882–3 *Little Ann and Other Poems* by Jane and Ann Taylor. Illustrations by Kate Greenaway. Printed by Edmund Evans in 1881, published in 1883 (George Routledge, London)

1883 *Almanack for 1883.* Four versions illustrated by Kate Greenaway (George Routledge, London)
A Calendar of the Months 1884. Illustrations by Kate Greenaway (Marcus Ward & Co, London)

Flowers and Fancies, Valentines Ancient and Modern by B. Montgomerie Ranking and Thomas K. Tully. Illustrations by Kate Greenaway (a revised edition of *The Quiver of Love*, 1876; Marcus Ward & Co, London)
Tales from the Edda by Helen Zimmern. Illustrations by Kate Greenaway and others (W. Swan Sonnenschein & Co, London)

1883–4 *Fors Clavigera* by John Ruskin. Illustrations by Kate Greenaway (George Allen, London and Orpington)

1884 *Almanack for 1884.* Illustrations by Kate Greenaway. Printed by Edmund Evans (George Routledge, London)
A Painting Book by Kate Greenaway (George Routledge, London)
Language of Flowers. Illustrations by Kate Greenaway, printed by Edmund Evans (George Routledge, London)
Songs for the Nursery. Collection of poems for children edited by Robert Ellice Mack. Illustrations by Kate Greenaway and others (W. Mack, London)

c.1884 *Kate Greenaway's Carols.* Issued as four pictorial cards with coloured figures, borders and music (George Routledge, London)

1885 *The English Spelling Book* by William Mavor. Illustrations by Kate Greenaway. Engraved and printed by Edmund Evans (George Routledge, London)
Almanack for 1885. Illustrations by Kate Greenaway (George Routledge, London)
Dame Wiggins of Lee and Her Seven Wonderful Cats by a lady of ninety with additional verses by John Ruskin. Four new illustrations by Kate Greenaway (George Allen, London and Orpington; a 6th edition was published in 1913)
Marigold Garden. Illustrations and rhymes by Kate Greenaway. Printed by Edmund Evans (George Routledge, London)

c.1885 *Kate Greenaway's Alphabet.* Each letter was a coloured illustration by Kate Greenaway (George Routledge, London; a reissue of the individual letters published in *The English Spelling Book,* 1885)
Kate Greenaway's Album. 192 coloured illustrations with gold borders, printed by Edmund Evans. One of the rarest Kate Greenaway books: only eight copies were printed, the book itself never being published (George Routledge, London)

1886 *Almanack for 1886.* Illustrations by Kate Greenaway (George Routledge, London)
A Apple Pie. Illustrations by Kate Greenaway, engraved and printed by Edmund Evans (originally one of Aunt Louisa's Toybooks, No 2, 1868, Frederick Warne, London; George Routledge, London)
The Queen of the Pirate Isle by Bret Harte. Illustrations by Kate Greenaway, engraved and printed by Edmund Evans (Chatto & Windus, London; American edition, 1887, Houghton Mifflin & Co, Boston and New York)

Baby's Birthday Book. Illustrations by Kate Greenaway and others (Marcus Ward & Co, London)

c.1886 *Rhymes for the Young Folk* by William Allingham. Illustrations by Kate Greenaway and others. Engraved and printed by Edmund Evans (Cassell & Co, London)

1887 *Almanack for 1887.* Illustrations by Kate Greenaway (George Routledge, London)
Queen Victoria's Jubilee Garland. Illustrations by Kate Greenaway. Printed by Edmund Evans (George Routledge, London)

1888 *Orient Line Guide.* Edited by W.J. Loftie, illustrations by Kate Greenaway (Sampson, Low, Marston, Searle & Rivington, London)
Almanack for 1888. Illustrations by Kate Greenaway (George Routledge, London)
The Pied Piper of Hamelin by Robert Browning. Illustrations by Kate Greenaway. Engraved and printed by Edmund Evans (George Routledge, London)
Around the House. Stories and poems with illustrations by Kate Greenaway taken from *Little Folks, The Illustrated London News,* etc, (Worthington & Co, New York)

1889 *Almanack for 1889.* Illustrations by Kate Greenaway; the designs were borrowed from the letters from *Kate Greenaway's Alphabet,* 1885 (George Routledge, London)
Kate Greenaway's Book of Games. Illustrations by Kate Greenaway, engraved and printed by Edmund Evans (George Routledge, London)
The Royal Progress of King Pepito by Beatrice F. Cresswell. Illustrations by Kate Greenaway. Engraved and printed by Edmund Evans (The Society for Promoting Christian Knowledge, London)

1890 *Almanack for 1890.* Illustrations by Kate Greenaway. Engraved and printed by Edmund Evans (George Routledge, London)

1891 *Kate Greenaway's Almanack for 1891.* Illustrations by Kate Greenaway (George Routledge, London)

1892 *Kate Greenaway's Almanack for 1892.* Illustrations by Kate Greenaway (George Routledge, London)

1893 *Kate Greenaway's Almanack for 1893.* Illustrations by Kate Greenaway (George Routledge, London)

1894 *Kate Greenaway's Almanack for 1894.* Illustrations by Kate Greenaway from *The English Spelling Book,* 1885 (George Routledge, London)

1895 *Kate Greenaway's Almanack for 1895.* Illustrations by Kate Greenaway (George Routledge, London)

1896 *Kate Greenaway's Calendar for 1897.* Illustrations by Kate Greenaway (George Routledge, London)

1897 *Kate Greenaway's Almanack and Diary for 1897* (J.M. Dent & Co, London)

1898 *Kate Greenaway's Calendar for 1899* (George Routledge, London)

1900 *The April Baby's Book of Tunes with the Story of How They Came to be Written* by Countess von Arnim. Illustrations by Kate Greenaway (Macmillan, London; also issued in 1900 by Macmillan, New York)

More charted design books by Julie Hasler

Cats and Kittens Charted Designs (Dover Publications, New York)
Kate Greenaway Alphabet Charted Designs (Dover Publications, New York)
Dogs and Puppies in Cross Stitch (Blandford Press, London)
Wild Flowers in Cross Stitch (Blandford Press, London)

INDEX

Figures in *italic* denote illustrations

Acetate, clear, 86, 101
Aida, 28, 56, 61, 86, 107
Ainring, 16, 56, 76, 113

Backing, 28, 29, 76, 86, 97
Bibliography, 118–19
Blouse, 9
Board, mounting, 56, 61
Bo-Peep, 56, 65, *66*
Boys, *77,* 85–8, *86,* 102
Butterflies, 45, *47*

Cards, 81, 86
  Greetings, 81–5, *82–3*
Child, 84, 105
  with butterflies, 45, *47*
  with hoop, 33, *35, 37, 39,* 41,
    43, 44, *46*
Cotton, stranded, 10, 12, 14, 16,
  28, 56, 61, 76, 81, 86, 92, 97,
  101, 104, 107, 113
Crochet, 10
Cushions, 8, 16–19, *18–19*

Dancing on the beach, 62, *63*
Dividers, 28
Duck, 21, *23*

Elastic, 113, 114

Fabric, 10, 12, 14, 113 *see also*
  individual headings
Finishing, 13, 29
Frames, miniature, 86
Framing, 61

Garland, 105
Girls, 32, *34,* 52–5, *55,* 57,
  58, 80, 84–6, 88, 89, 102,
  116–17
Greenaway, Kate, 6–7, 118–19

Hardanger, 81, 101, 104
Hardida, 92
Hoop, 33, *35, 37, 39,* 41, *43,* 44,
  46, 102
  embroidery, 10, 12

Jam-pot covers, 97–100, *98–9*
Jump for Joy, 59–61, *59*

Kapok, 76
Kite, 84
Knitting, 10
Knots, 12

Lace, 15–17, 76, 97
Lady with dog, 25, *27*
  with parasol, 36. *38*
Lamb, 20, *22*
Lavender, 76
  bags, 8, 76–81, *78–9*
Linda, 61, 97
Lining, 107, 112
Lugana, 101

Maids, 24, *26*
Making up, 76, 81, 107, 112
Miniatures, 86–91, *90–1*
Mounting, 61

Needlepoint, 10
Needles, 10
Nightdress bag, 107–12, *110–11*

Oversewing, 15, *15,* 17

Paperweights, 81, 104–6, *106*
Pictures, 8, 9, 56–75 *see also*
  individual headings
Poem, 107, 109
Polly Flinders, 61, 68–75, *70–1,*
  74–5

Pressing, 14, 16, 28, 29, 61, 76,
  81, 97, 112, 114

Quilt, cot, 8, 9, 28–31, *30–1*

Ribbon, 76, 97, 107, 112

Satin, 16
Scissors, 10
Seam allowance, 16, 17, 28, 76,
  107, 113, 114
Skirt, 8, 9, 113–17, *115*
Skipping, 48, *50*
Sponge, 101
Stick, 37, *39*
Stitches, 12–15
  back, 13, 14, 61, 107
  basting, 12, 15, *15,* 29
  catch, 17
  cross, 8, 12–13, *13*
  running, 14, *14,* 29
  slip, 15, *15,* 29
  whip, 15, *15*
Suppliers, 119

Tablecloth, 92–6, *94–5*
Tape, adhesive, 81
  masking, 12, 56, 61
Template, 86, 97, 104
Tension, 12
Threads, 10, 12, 14 *see also*
  cotton, stranded
Tom Tucker, 56, 64, *67*
Toy on a rope, 40, *42*
Trinket boxes, 8, 101–3, *103*

Wadding, 15, 28, 29
Walking, 49, *51*
Windmill, 52, *54,* 86–8
Workbasket, *11*

DEDICATION

This book is dedicated to my partner
in life, my biggest supporter, my
harshest critic, my balance, my love —

my wife Sylvia.

ACKNOWLEDGEMENTS

My thanks to Elliott Wolf and Peanut Butter Publishing
for their guidance in making this project a reality, in
particular Diana Douglas, organizer and editor supreme.
The book design artist, Fiona Raven, has contributed
greatly in making this book user friendly and effective.
The illustrations give life to a difficult subject, thanks to
our artist, Susie Morris. Thank you all.

PREFACE

If you watch my TV show "Everyday Workout" you have been using some of Dr. Steven Stark's techniques already! As the host of one of North America's top exercise programs, my audience expects me to give them the correct information about stretching.

I use many of the techniques Dr. Stark presents in *The Stark Reality of Stretching* consistently with my viewers. There are many misconceptions about how muscles work and how to best keep our body tuned and lessen potential injuries. This book not only describes how your lower body works but also why stretching the wrong way can actually contribute to more exercise problems.

As a former patient and convert to his methods, I strongly recommend this book for everyone — from the casual walker to professional athletes. Please tell your friends about it and have fun stretching and exercising the right way for many years to come.

Best of life, lungs and leg-lifts

Cynthia Kereluk

Cynthia Kereluk is North America's #1-ranked female television exercise host. Her show "Everyday Workout" has aired internationally since 1985. This former Miss Canada has a degree in education from Simon Fraser University.

TABLE OF CONTENTS ·······················

Acknowledgements iv
Preface v
Introduction xiv

Section 1   Structure: How we are designed
Function: How we move

Chapter 1   4 – 17

Anatomical Structures

I.   Joints 4
   A. Definition 5
   B. Purpose 5
   C. Potential Injuries 5
II.   Connective Tissue 6
   A. Composition of Connective Tissue 6
   B. Types of Connective Tissue 7
     (a) Tendons 7
     (b) Ligaments 10
     (c) Fascia 13
III.   Skeletal Muscle Anatomy 14
   A. Definition 14
   B. Structure 16

Chapter 2   18 – 25

How Muscles Function

  I.   Pathways of Neuromuscular Control   19
    A. Voluntary Contractions   19
    B. Involuntary (Reflex) Contractions   19
    C. Types of Contractions   21
      (a) Shortening (concentric) contractions   21
      (b) Lengthening (eccentric) contractions   22
      (c) Holding (isometric) contractions   23
    D. Resting Length   24
    E. How Muscles Use Energy   25

Chapter 3   26 – 30

How Muscles "Stretch"

  I.   Definition of a "Stretch"   27
 II.   Mechanism of Stretching   28
    A. Initial Contraction   29
    B. Relaxation   29
    C. Sliding Elongation   29
III.   Maximum Length of Sarcomeres   30

Chapter 4   31 – 32

Properties of Muscles

  I.   Muscle Strength   31
 II.   Muscle Power   32

Chapter 5   33 – 38

Benefits of Stretching

I.	Benefits for Athletes: Performance	33
II.	Benefits for Children	35
III.	Benefits for Everyone	36
	A. Maintaining Proper Muscle Length &	
	Symmetry in the Lower Extremity	36
	B. Relaxation of Muscle	38
IV.	Prevention of Injuries	38

Chapter 6   39 – 42

Summary

Section 2   Muscle Preparation
How to Stretch
Mistakes in Stretching

Chapter 7   44 – 53

Preparing to Stretch:
Proper Warm-up Exercises

I.	Definition	44
II.	Types of Warm-ups	46
	A. Walking	46
	B. Gentle Power Movements with Light Weights	46
	C. Other Warm-up Exercises	47
III.	Incorrect Warm-ups	48
IV.	Mechanisms of Shock Absorption	48
	A. Muscle Function	49
	B. Joint Range of Motion	51
	C. Horizontal Displacement of the Body Mass	51
V.	Summary	53

Chapter 8   54 – 55

Primary Stretches and Skill-level Stretches

I. Primary Stretches   54
II. Skill-level Stretches   55

Chapter 9   56 – 58

How to Stretch

Chapter 10   59 – 62

The 5 Golden Rules of Stretching

I.   Isolate the Muscle Group   59
II. Find Zero Tension   60
III. Find the First Awareness   60
IV. Less is Best   61
V.   Allow the Loss of Tension   61

Chapter 11   63 – 72

Mistakes in Stretching

I.   Timing   64
     A. How long to hold any one stretch   64
     B. When to stretch   65
II. Positioning   66
III. Loading other Structures   66
IV. Overstretching   68
V.   Good Soreness/Bad Soreness   70
     A. Good Soreness   70
     B. Bad Soreness   72

Chapter 12   73 – 80

Stretching Techniques

I.	Dynamic Stretches	74
II.	PNF Stretches	75
III.	Passive-active and Active-assisted Stretches	78
IV.	Static Stretches	78

Section 3 Primary Stretches for the Major Weight-bearing Muscle Groups of the Lower Extremity

Chapter 13   83 – 110

Calf Muscles (Gastrocnemius and Soleus Muscles)

I.	Gastrocnemius Muscle	84
	A. Anatomy	84
	B. Biomechanics	85
	C. Normal Gait Cycle	85
II.	Midstance Phase of the Normal Gait Cycle	86
	A. Pronation	86
	B. Resupination	87
III.	Structural Damage Caused by Shortened Calf Muscles	89
	A. Stress on the Ligaments of the Lower Extremity	89
	B. Bunions	91
	C. Asymmetry	92
IV.	Gastrocnemius Stretch: Both Legs at the Same Time	94
	A. Advantages of stretching both gastrocnemius muscles at the same time	97
IV.	Gastrocnemius Stretch: One Leg at a Time	98

V.	Mistakes in the Gastrocnemius Muscle Stretch	100
	A. Overstretching	100
	B. Positioning Errors	102
	C. Loading Other Structures	104
VI.	Soleus Muscle	108
	A. Anatomy	108
VII.	Soleus Stretch	109
VIII.	Mistakes in the Soleus Muscle Stretch	110
	A. Positioning Errors	110

Chapter 14   111 – 122

Groin Muscles (Adductors)

I.	Groin Muscles (Adductors)	112
	A. Anatomy	112
	B. Biomechanics	112
II.	Sitting Groin Stretch: (Sitting Adductor Stretch)	114
III.	Mistakes in Groin Stretches	117
	A. Overstretching	117
	B. Ballistics or Pushing On The Legs	118
	C. Loading Other Structures	118
	(a) Ligaments of the Pelvis	118
	(b) Ligaments of the Spine	119
	D. Positioning Errors	120

Chapter 15   123 – 132

Quadriceps

I.	Quadriceps	124
	A. Anatomy	124
	B. Biomechanics	124
II.	Quadriceps Stretch: Lying on Your Side	126
III.	Standing Quadriceps Stretch	128
IV.	Mistakes in Quadriceps Stretches	129

A. Positioning Errors 129
B. Loading Other Structures 129
C. Injuries 131

Chapter 16   133 – 150

Hamstrings

   I.   Hamstrings 134
       A. Anatomy 134
       B. Biomechanics 134
  II.   Sitting Hamstring Stretch 136
 III.   Hamstring Stretches Lying on the Back .. 139
 IV.   The Wall Stretch 141
  V.   Isolating the Medial or Lateral Hamstrings .. 142
 VI.   Mistakes in Hamstring Stretches 144
       A. Positioning Errors 144
       B. Loading Other Structures 145
       C. Incorrect Positioning Due to
           Involuntary Muscle Contraction ... 147
         (a) All Standing Hamstring Stretches .. 147
         (b) Ballet Bar Stretches 149

Chapter 17   151 – 164

Posterior Hip Muscles
(Gluteus Maximus and
the External Hip Rotators)

   I.   Gluteus Maximus Muscle 152
       A. Anatomy 152
       B. Biomechanics 152
  II.   External Hip Rotator Muscles 154
       A. Anatomy 154
       B. Biomechanics 154

III.   Relationship of the Posterior Hip Muscles
and the Sciatic Nerve Roots   156
IV.   Gluteus Maximus and
External Hip Rotator Stretch   159
V.   Mistakes in Posterior Hip Muscle Stretches   162
    A. Overstretching   162
    B. Positioning Errors   162
    C. Loading Other Structures   163

Chapter 18   165–174

Hip Flexors
(Psoas and the Iliacus Muscles)

I.   Psoas and Iliacus Muscles   166
    A. Anatomy   166
        (a) Psoas Muscle   166
        (b) Iliacus Muscle   168
    B. Biomechanics   168
II.   Hip Flexor Stretch   170
    A. Stretching Alone   170
    B. Stretching with a Partner   172

Section 4   Easy Reference to Correct Stretches

I.   Gastrocnemius Stretch:
Both Legs at the Same Time   176
II.   Sitting Groin Stretch: (Sitting Adductor Stretch)   178
III.   Quadriceps Stretch: Lying on Your Side   180
IV.   Sitting Hamstring Stretch   182
V.   Gluteus Maximus and
External Hip Rotator Stretch   184

Glossary   187
Bibliography   198

INTRODUCTION

As an athlete I was always fascinated by how people moved. Watching people as they exercised and trained for a specific sport was an education in the diversity of the human body.

I found it curious that athletes with similar body appearance and muscle development often had different stride lengths and varying capabilities. I began to question why some people with fairly lean muscle development had more power than those with larger, more defined muscle groups. It appeared that athletes with larger muscles were stronger and could lift more weight, but the athlete with the leaner muscles could run faster and jump higher.

My interest grew to the point where the study of these issues led to a career as a physician. Although I completed a three-year surgical residency program after medical school, I have since dedicated my practice to focus on prevention and healing before the need for surgery. I am now a podiatric physician specializing in sports medicine and functional control. My expertise is in the structure and function of the lower extremities.

Every day in my office I see patients who are in pain:

- Teenagers, good athletes and non-athletes alike, whose most common symptom is knee pain.
- Adults who want to be more active but can't because of chronic and slowly increasing problems such as knee pain, lowback pain, or plantar fasciitis.
- Seniors who may or may not have exercised throughout their life, and who are now suffering aches and pains which are attributed to "old age."

Why do so many teenagers who are basically healthy have knee pain and poor posture at such a young age?

Why do we all seem to have increasing problems with joint pain and postural changes as we get older, regardless of how hard we try to stay healthy?

The study of the human gait cycle, the proper sequence of *joint motion* and *phasic muscle activity* during walking or running, has led to an understanding of how *muscle imbalances* cause ligament stress and joint damage in everyone.

It also explains why so many people have these problems simply doing normal daily activities without any sports involvement.

Muscle imbalances develop because the *weight bearing muscles of the lower extremity* gradually shorten over time with *repetitive usage* and *fatigue*. These large muscles will remain shortened for the rest of our lives if stretches are not done routinely and correctly.

What to do? The answer seems obvious. Everyone should include stretches for the lower extremity muscles in their daily life. Indeed, many people do stretch faithfully. However, many of these people are stretching incorrectly. They gain no benefit, and often cause permanent damage to various structures of the body.

The tremendous growth of the fitness industry has overwhelmed us with personal trainers in the fitness clubs, articles in magazines and newspapers, TV shows and video tapes on exercise and stretching. How can we distinguish between good information and bad? Where do we find current scientific facts, not personal opinions, in plain language anyone can understand and apply?

There has been an abundance of research done on how muscles function and the differences in the structure and function of muscles, tendons, and ligaments. However, this scientific data was hard to find and usually focused on the individual structures at the MOLECULAR LEVEL. This made the information too technical to be understood and translated into practical application by the average person.

We have operating manuals for our cars, VCRs, CD players — virtually everything in our lives EXCEPT OUR BODIES.

The Stark Reality Of Stretching is a comprehensive operator's manual for the body. It provides the science, the anatomy, precise definitions, and the illustrations necessary for the proper application of that knowledge to help keep the body healthy throughout our lifetime.

The Stark Reality of Stretching provides a current and concise understanding of why we should stretch, WHAT A STRETCH IS, and of course how to stretch properly. We hope that you use this book in good health!

How To Use This Book

The book is divided into four sections:

Section 1

contains the science that is necessary to explain the differences in muscles, tendons, and ligaments. This section is vital to anyone who wishes to truly understand muscle function. Understanding muscle contractions and how a muscle elongates during a stretch at the molecular level will dispel many of the myths that we have all grown up with. Accurate definitions are essential for anyone trying to instruct other people on how to exercise and stretch without injury.

Section 2

contains a summary of related topics necessary for a total picture of proper training. Included are discussions on proper warm-up exercises, how to stretch, mistakes in stretches, and a summary of the most prevalent theories on stretching.

Section 3

is the application of the knowledge gained in Sections 1 and 2. Each major muscle group of the lower extremity is examined. The anatomy, biomechanics, and proper primary stretches are explained. Important landmarks for each muscle group are illustrated. In addition, the most common mistakes made in stretching each of these muscle groups is described, and the structures that can be damaged by these errors are illustrated.

Section 4

is a quick-reference guide to proper stretches. It provides simple instructions and illustrations for the best primary stretch of any selected muscle group.

Glossary

The glossary contains as many of the terms of anatomy, biomechanics, and function as possible in order for you to review the meaning of a term or definition without having to remember where in the book you first encountered that term.

Bibliography

Throughout the book specific references are provided in shaded text boxes. These references cite the author and the date only. For example: (Ramachandran, 1967).

For the complete reference simply find this author and date in the alphabetically listed bibliography.

Illustrations

All of the illustrations in this book are original, and are meant to highlight the important anatomical landmarks and structures, as well as demonstrate good and bad stretching positions in a manner easily understood by everyone.

SECTION 1

STRUCTURE: How we are designed

FUNCTION: How we move

Our bodies are exquisite in design and function. Every structure in our bodies is customized for a specific purpose. For example, the knee joint bends (flexes) and straightens (extends) to make our legs more mobile. The muscles whose tendons cross the knee joint produce the motion across the joint. The ligaments stabilize the joint and prevent the joint from being dislocated or injured by abnormal motion.

Proper stretching allows maximum benefits for both health and performance. This reduces the risk of potentially painful and debilitating injury to muscle and connective tissue. Stretching requires an understanding of the body structure and how it functions.

The Stark Reality of Stretching deals exclusively with the structures of the lower extremities. The following topics will be discussed with the aid of illustrations.

Chapter 1 Anatomical Structures

    I.   Joints

    II. Connective Tissues

    III. Skeletal Muscle Anatomy

Chapter 2 How Muscles Function

    I.   Pathways of Neuromuscular Control

    II. Types of Contractions

        A. Shortening contractions (concentric contractions)

        B. Lengthening contractions (eccentric contractions)

        C. Holding contractions (isometric contractions)

    III. Resting Length (current and best resting length)

    IV. How Muscles use Energy

Chapter 3 How Muscles "Stretch"

 I. Definition of a "Stretch"

 II. Mechanism of Stretching

 III. Maximum Sarcomere Length

Chapter 4 Properties of Muscles

 I. Muscle Strength

 II. Muscle Power

Chapter 5 Benefits of Stretching

 I. Benefits for Athletes

 II. Benefits for Children

 III. Benefits for Everyone

 IV. Prevention of Injuries

Chapter 6 Summary

Chapter 1

ANATOMICAL STRUCTURES

I. JOINTS

Essentially, there are three types of joints:

1. Extremely stable and virtually immovable joints, like the cranium.
2. Slightly movable joints, like the spinal column.
3. Freely movable or synovial joints, like the knee and ankle.

The joints of the lower extremities are: the hip, knee, ankle, and the many joints of the foot. All of these joints are synovial joints.

A. Definition JOINTS

Joints are places of union or junction between two bones to allow motion. The two bones are joined together by ligaments, and there is articular cartilage between the bones to provide the smooth surface to allow gliding motion.

B. Purpose JOINTS

Joints allow motion in order to provide mobility for the body.

- Joint stability is provided by the ligaments that connect the two bones and limit abnormal motion of the joint; by the shape of the joint and by other connective tissues such as the joint capsules.

- Joint motion is produced by the muscles and their tendons that cross the joint.

C. Potential Injuries JOINTS

Stable joints, like the hips, provide limited movement whereas less stable joints, like the wrist, allow a wide range of motion. Although less stable joints are more easily damaged, all joints and their connective tissues can be harmed when they are forced beyond their normal range of motion.

II. CONNECTIVE TISSUE

Tendons, ligaments and fascia are comprised of connective tissue. Connective tissue is a mixture of collagenous and elastin fibers. Connective tissues are the fibrous cords that bind the individual body structures together. The differences in structure and function of collagen and elastin are very important. These differences are explained below.

A. Composition of Connective Tissue

Connective tissue is made up of two kinds of fibers: collagenous and elastic fibers.

- Collagenous fibers, rich in protein, are essentially *non-elastic*.
- Elastic fibers are characterized by the presence of the elastin protein. These fibers can be stretched, and when tension is relaxed will shorten again. They are combined with the more numerous collagenous fibers in varying amounts in connective tissue. The increased elasticity of specific ligaments and muscle fascia results from an increased percentage of elastin protein mixed with the collagen fibers.

The greatest proportion of tissue in tendons, ligaments, and fascia is collagenous fibers. The amount of elastin fibers in these structures varies with the purpose of the structure. Tendons are almost totally collagen fibers because they are not meant to stretch, while the muscle fascia has a higher concentration of elastin fibers so that it can elongate and contract.

As a person grows older, the elasticity of the connective tissue tends to deteriorate. This tendency is accelerated by inactivity, *postural malalignment* and *muscular imbalance.*

B. Types of Connective Tissue

(a) Tendons

Definition and Purpose

Tendons are the most *inelastic connective tissue* in the body. They are the tough connective tissue that attach muscle to bone. All muscles have a tendon of origin (where they originate from a bone) and a tendon of insertion (where the other end attaches by tendon to bone). The tendon of origin is usually attached to the more stable bone, while the tendon of insertion is attached to the more moveable bone.

Tendons consist almost entirely of heavy, inelastic collagen fibers that are stronger than both the muscle and the bone covering (periosteum) that the tendon attaches to.

Potential Injuries TENDONS

Tendons can be partially torn or completely ruptured if loaded beyond their tensile strength. However, since the tendon has a higher tensile strength than the muscle or the bone covering (periosteum), most excessive loads on the tendon result in tearing of the muscle tissue or the periosteum of the bone.

This means that **TENDON CANNOT BE STRETCHED**. Composed of inelastic collagen fibers, a weight of ten thousand times the molecular weight of the tendon will not stretch the tendon (Verzar, 1963).

Research indicates that microscopic fibers of tendons can be stretched to a maximum of approximately 10% of their original length before they rupture. However, at the molecular level, the fibers (protofibrils) of the tendon undergo an extension of only about 3% (Ramachandran, 1967).

In another study, a stress of 4% was significant and corresponds to the limit of reversibility, and therefore of elasticity. At this point, the tendon's surface waviness disappears, and if the stretch continues injury may result (Crisp, 1972)

Acute Injury TENDONS

The healthy tendon will not rupture with a major overload. Instead, the muscle belly will tear or rupture and separate from the tendon; and the tendon may tear the periosteum of the bone the tendon is attached to.

A classic example of this major overload is tearing the patella tendon (tendon avulsion) completely off the front of the shin bone (the tibial tuberosity) while jumping. Several NFL football players and NBA basketball players have suffered this type of functional injury.

Chronic Injury TENDONS

Overstretching of muscle places a heavy load on the tendon. Since the tendon is *inelastic* (the *maximum* increase in length of the actual fibers of the tendon can only be 3 – 4%), what often results is a microscopic tearing of the muscle tissue or of the bone covering (periosteum).

The most common cause of damage and degeneration of tendons is extended stress due to postural faults, poor biomechanics, extended overuse, and excessive tightness in the muscle of that tendon.

(b) Ligaments

Definition and Purpose

Ligaments are tough connective tissues that stabilize and reinforce joints by connecting bone to bone. They consist of almost pure collagenous fiber. The amount of elasticity is again determined by the amount of elastin protein the ligaments contain.

The ligaments of the spine and the foot contain the most elastin content, which is why they are the most elastic ligaments in the body. They are therefore the easiest to damage with over-extension.

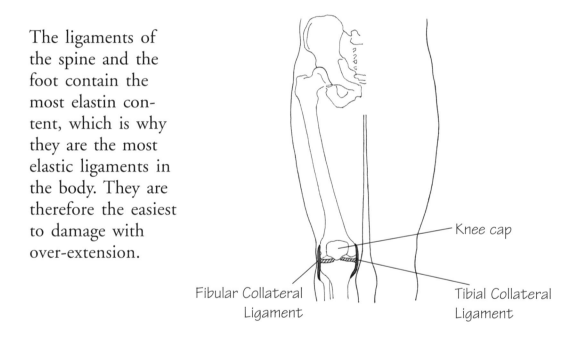

Collateral Ligaments of the Knee

The degree of elasticity in ligaments also varies with gender (in general, women have more ligament elasticity than men), age, and the level of physical fitness.

Potential Injuries LIGAMENTS

Although they are pliant and flexible, nearly all ligaments lose their ability to perform correctly when they are elongated by chronic over-extension. This is explained by the elastic and plastic properties of ligaments.

Elastic Deformity LIGAMENTS
from Acute Overload

When a joint is forced into an abnormal position during movement, the ligament has an abnormal stress applied to it. The ligament can withstand enormous forces for a very brief time. If the force is not removed, or if it exceeds the tensile strength of the ligament, then the ligament tears or ruptures. This is an elastic deformity caused by acute or sudden overload.

A classic example of this is the ankle sprain (inversion injury of the ankle). Most of these injuries are tears or complete ruptures of one or more ligaments on the lateral aspect of the ankle joint. These injuries are more severe than commonly thought, and should have immediate and proper treatment with current therapy. It takes from eight to twelve weeks to regain tensile strength in a damaged ligament, and the joint must be protected during this period with taping or with a brace.

The torn part of the ligament heals by bridging the torn fibers with scar tissue (fibrosis). The ligament will always be slightly longer and less effective in stopping abnormal joint motion, and the scar tissue will never be as strong as the original tissue. This is often the site of more tearing, chronic weakness, and repeated injury.

Plastic Deformity from Chronic Overload

When a ligament is put under a continuous and protracted stress it will gradually elongate. This is called *plastic deformity*. A classic example is the damage done to the medial collateral ligaments of the knee in the incorrect "hurdler's stretch." This is explained in the section on Hamstring stretches on page 145, Section 3.

Medial Collateral
Ligament Damage

As the ligament elongates it becomes weaker, and the joint that should be stabilized by the ligament has abnormal motion (hypermobility) because the stretched ligament no longer binds the bones of the joint properly. This joint hypermobility results in chronic inflammation which may lead to degenerative arthritis.

All ligaments can be permanently elongated if subjected to protracted stress from postural faults, poor biomechanics, or *repetitive overstretching* beyond their tensile strength.

(c) Fascia

Definition and Purpose

Fascia is the connective tissue which forms enveloping sheaths around the entire muscle and each individual muscle bundle (fasciculi).

Fascia consists principally of *collagenous fibers,* although the amount of elastic fibers varies with the functional activity of the muscle. The large muscles of the extremities have a limited amount of elastic tissue.

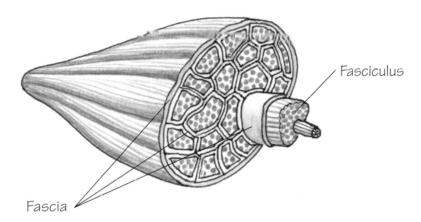

Fasciculus

Fascia

Potential Injuries

Fascia resist very high momentary tension stresses during body movement without rupturing. Protracted stress will result in permanent elongation. Fascia also has a strong tendency to shorten due to age, cold, poor posture, and *muscular imbalance.* This long-term shortening of the fascia shortens the muscle, reducing the range of motion across the joints of the body.

III. SKELETAL MUSCLE ANATOMY

There are three main types of muscle — skeletal muscle, smooth muscle (found in the internal organs) and heart muscle. In *The Stark Reality of Stretching* we are concerned with skeletal muscles of the lower extremity: how they function, and how they stretch.

A. Definition

Skeletal muscles are the voluntary contractile tissues that move our skeletons about. They are attached directly via tendons to bones. There are more than *600* skeletal muscles in the body. These differ in size and shape according to their function.

There are six main muscle groups in the lower extremities that produce or stabilize motion:

1. the hip flexors
2. the muscles of the posterior hip (the gluteal muscles and external hip rotators)
3. the quadriceps
4. the hamstrings
5. the groin muscles (the adductors)
6. the calf muscles.

Each of these muscles or muscle groups has tendons that cross a joint. The contractions of the muscles provide the movement of the joints.

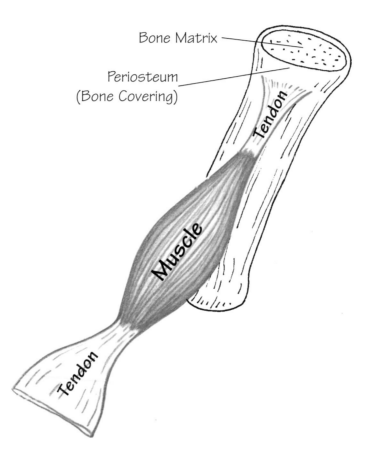

Bone Matrix

Periosteum
(Bone Covering)

Tendon

Muscle

Tendon

This diagram illustrates that all skeletal muscle originates from a tendon, and the tendon attaches to the periosteum of the bone.

B. Structure

- Muscles are made up of bundles called *fasciculi.*
- The fasciculi are made up of a group of muscle fibers composed of *myofibrils.*
- Myofibrils are made up of *sarcomeres.*
- Sarcomeres are made up of *myofilaments.*
- Myofilaments are made up of units of overlapping proteins called *myosin* and *actin.*

Myosin molecules have a long rod-shaped tail, a shorter rod-shaped neck, and two globular heads which form the cross bridges that connect to the actin protein and produce the motion required for contraction of the muscle.

The action of the cross bridging and the energy cycle of muscle contraction is important. However, the molecular level of muscle function is very technical, and beyond the scope of this book. The purpose of this book is to give athletes, coaches, everyone, an accurate understanding of muscle function and stretching that has a practical application and that translates easily when taught to others.

How muscles function, the properties of muscles, and how muscles stretch are the subjects of the next chapters.

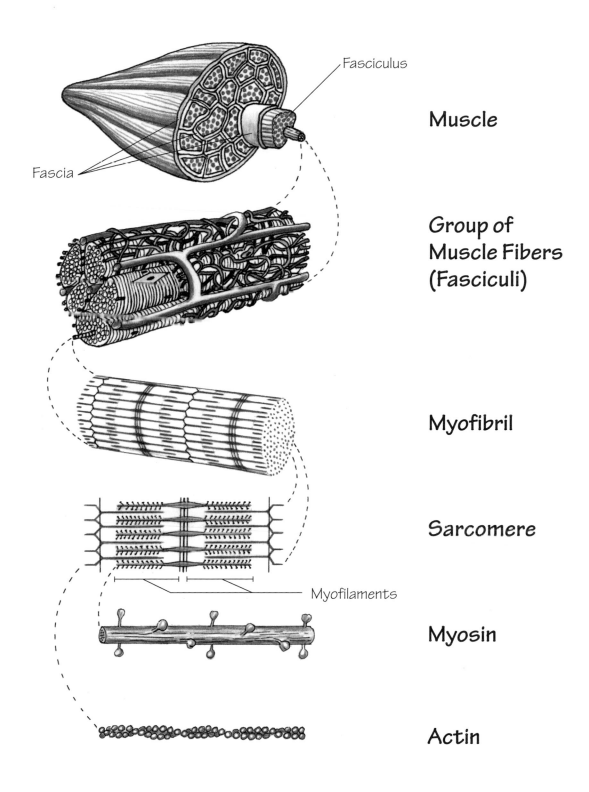

Fasciculus

Muscle

Fascia

Group of
Muscle Fibers
(Fasciculi)

Myofibril

Sarcomere

Myofilaments

Myosin

Actin

Chapter 2

HOW MUSCLES FUNCTION

Muscles shorten and elongate in order to produce motion across a joint, or they contract without changing length to hold a body position. It is important to understand the different pathways nerves can use to produce contractions of the muscle in order to appreciate what a stretch is, and how to accomplish the stretch.

Skeletal muscle contractions are either conscious *voluntary* contractions when using the muscles to lift or move an object intentionally, or *involuntary* contractions when the muscles contract in response to a loading force without conscious thought.

I. Pathways of Neuromuscular Control

A. Voluntary Contractions

When a person lifts the lower leg using the hamstring muscles, the brain (upper motor neurons) sends a message (nerve impulse) down the spinal cord to the anterior horn cells (lower motor neurons). The nerve impulse then travels from the spinal cord to the muscle fibers (the motor end plates). This nerve impulse causes the hamstring muscles to contract in order to produce motion and lift the leg. This is an example of the brain directing muscle contractions to produce conscious functions.

B. Involuntary (Reflex) Contractions

When a person bends forward from the waist in a standing position, the hamstrings contract to stabilize the pelvis against gravity. If the hamstrings relaxed, the person would inevitably fall forward. The person does not think about contracting the hamstrings, and **CANNOT RELAX** the hamstrings while in this position.

This is an example of a reflex contraction in response to gravity and balance; also known as a *myotactic or proprioceptive reflex contraction.* The lower motor neurons are the anterior and posterior horn cells of the spinal cord. They are located throughout the spinal cord wherever the large nerve roots leave the spinal cord to enter the body.

This reflex contraction starts with a lengthening load on the hamstrings as the person leans forward. The nerve fibers in the muscle (*the muscle spindles*) react to the new load and lengthening caused by the forward bending. The muscle spindles send myotatic nerve impulses to the spinal cord (posterior horn cells), which direct the impulses to the anterior horn cells of the spinal cord, which route the impulses directly back to the motor end plates of the muscle causing an *involuntary contraction of the muscle.* This is a "loop" of nerve cells from the muscle into the "back door" of the spinal cord, passed on through the "front door" of the spinal cord back to the muscles, causing them to contract.

There is no brain function (*upper motor neuron*) involved in the initial contraction of the hamstrings to stabilize the pelvis.

The involuntary contraction of the hamstrings continues in order to maintain a specific postural position against the pull of gravity. The involuntary contraction is maintained by the myotactic reflex caused by the proprioceptive sensors of the muscles and brain. This becomes very important in the discussion on positioning in proper stretches.

C. Types of Contractions

All types of muscle contractions explained below can be caused by either voluntary or involuntary neuromuscular pathways.

(a) Shortening (concentric) contractions are when:

A muscle develops tension sufficient to overcome a resistance and produce work, causing the muscle to visibly shorten and move a body part against that resistance. In all of the individual myofilaments, the actin protein moves over the myosin and all the myofilaments shorten, expend energy, and *produce motion*.

Myofilament shortening from Resting Length to Maximum Contraction

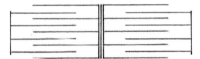 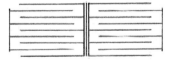

Best Resting Length   Partial Contraction   Maximum Contraction

Example: When you lift your leg using the hamstring muscles, the individual myofilaments are shortening. The actin protein fibers are sliding over the myosin protein fibers. The myofilaments shorten from their *current resting length* to their *maximum contracted length*. The muscle is expending energy and producing motion. This is a concentric contraction of the muscle.

(b) Lengthening (eccentric) contractions are when:

A specific resistance or load overcomes the muscle tension and the muscle actually lengthens. In this case the muscle does negative work. In all of the individual myofilaments, the actin protein moves away from the myosin protein and all the myofilaments lengthen. The muscle as a whole lengthens, expends energy, and *controls motion.*

Myofilament elongating from Maximum Contraction to Resting Length

Maximum Contraction   Partial Contraction   Best Resting Length

Example: When you lower your leg the hamstrings are elongating. The actin protein fibers are sliding over the myosin and the myofilaments are elongating. The muscle is expanding energy and *controlling motion.* This is an eccentric contraction.

(c) Holding (isometric) contractions are when:

The muscle develops tension insufficient to move a body part against a given resistance and the length of the muscle remains unchanged. The myofilaments are not changing length, and the muscle is *expending energy and doing work* to maintain that position. There is no motion in the joint.

Myofilament partially contracted, expending energy, not changing length

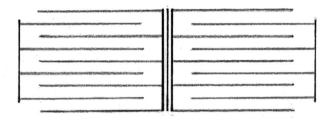

Partial Contraction

Example: When you hold the leg partially raised without movement using the hamstring muscles to stabilize this position. The hamstrings are expending energy to maintain that position, but the myofilaments are not changing length.

D. Resting Length
(current resting length and best resting length)

The muscle fibers are at their resting length when the muscles are not expending energy or doing work.

At their *best resting length possible* in human muscle tissue, the myofilaments are only 25% longer than their maximally contracted length.

Best Resting Length

The current resting length for most adults remains fairly constant in the non-weight-bearing muscles of the arms, but varies greatly in the weight-bearing muscles of the lower extremity.

For most people their current resting length is NOT their best resting length in the weight-bearing muscles of the lower extremity. This is a direct result of years of gradual shortening of the weight-bearing muscles due to repetitive motion (e.g., walking) and due to a lack of proper stretches (not extending the muscles back to the best resting length after exercise).

Most people are NOT starting their activity or sport at their best resting length. The overlapping protein fibers of weight bearing muscles have shortened in their overlap, and the surrounding connective tissue (myofascia) has shortened due to years of *not being extended back to the best resting length after exercise or repetitive motion.*

E. How Muscles Use Energy

When a muscle is doing work, it is expending energy to accomplish that work, whether the muscle is shortening, elongating, or maintaining a steady length while resisting the tension of the load placed on it.

- Muscles expend energy and shorten to produce motion.

- Muscles expend energy and elongate to control motion.

- Muscles expend energy without changing length, resisting motion, in order to maintain a position.

- Muscles store energy (e.g., during a stretch).

- Muscles will dissipate the energy stored during a stretch as heat if the muscles are not utilized within a certain period of time after the stretch.

Chapter 3

HOW MUSCLES STRETCH

Unfortunately the terminology of "stretching" that we have all grown up with is misleading. When we understand the mechanisms of this muscle function, it becomes clear that nothing really stretches.

The term "stretch" leads people to think this is something they can make happen, instead of something they have to *allow* to happen.

I. Definition of a "Stretch"

A stretch is a *sliding elongation* of the overlapping protein fibers (the actin and myosin proteins) of the myofilaments *past each other*. This results in a lengthening of the myofilaments *past their current resting length.*

The sarcomere length increases due to the elongation of the myofilaments. The myofilaments elongate because the actin and myosin protein fibers slide past each other. Neither the actin or the myosin protein fibers change length.

If a muscle or muscle group is *involuntarily contracted*, doing work and expending energy to maintain a position, the muscles cannot relax back to their resting length. The stretch, the sliding elongation of the muscle fibers past the current resting length, will never begin.

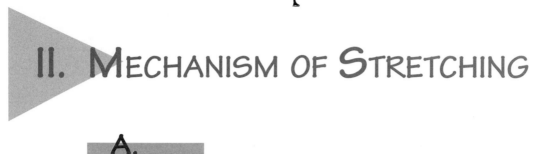

II. MECHANISM OF STRETCHING

A.

When any muscle or muscle group is initially loaded, the first thing that happens is a lower motor neuron reflex contraction. The relaxed muscles contract in response to the loading force. All of those millions of myofilaments shorten. At this point the muscle is contracted and expending energy to resist the initial force placed on the muscle.

B.

If the tension on the muscle is held long enough, in a position where the muscles can relax (i.e., it is not expending energy to maintain that position), and if the muscle is not overloaded, the muscle will relax back to its *original resting length.*

C.

Only then will the sliding elongation of those over-lapping protein fibers *past their original resting length occur.* The sliding elongation continues until there is no longer any tension on the muscle.

A. Initial Contraction

Best Resting Length

Partial Contraction

B. Relaxation

Partial Contraction

Best Resting Length

C. Sliding Elongation

Best Resting Length

Maximum Elongation **Past** the Best Resting Length

III. MAXIMUM LENGTH OF SARCOMERES

The myofilaments have a finite distance they can elongate through this sliding elongation. The actin protein *cannot* slide past the end of the myosin protein. The cross bridging must be maintained for muscle function.

Muscle fibers have a maximally contracted length, a best resting length, and a *maximum elongation past their best resting length*.

Maximum Contraction   Best Resting Length   Maximum Elongation **Past**
the Best Resting Length

A maximally contracted muscle fiber (myofilament) is approximately 25% shorter than its best resting length. At its longest possible length after stretching the myofilaments are *60-70% LONGER than at its best resting length*.

Chapter 4

PROPERTIES OF MUSCLES

I. MUSCLE STRENGTH

Strength is defined as "contractibility, the capacity to shorten and the ability to develop tension." Through exercise the number of individual muscle fibers (myofilaments) is increased. This increase in the mass of the muscle increases the muscle's ability to develop tension.

Strength is simply translated as how large the mass of the muscle is, how much load a muscle can *hold*, and how much *tension* the muscle can develop without tearing.

II. MUSCLE POWER

Power is defined as how much load a muscle can *move* and how *fast* that muscle can move a specific load. A muscle has its most *power* when the individual muscle fibers are at their longest length of contraction. That muscle can move a larger load at a faster speed. As the muscle fibers shorten (contract), the load they can move and/or the speed they can move that load decreases.

**This is what makes stretching
so vitally important to athletes!!!!!**

Pre-stretched muscle (stretching the muscle before the sports or activity) functions with greater efficiency because elastic energy is stored in the muscle tissue during stretching and is recovered during the subsequent shortening (Asmussen & Bonde-Petersin, 1974; Boscoe, Tarkka, & Komi, 1982; Cavagna, Dusman, & Margaria, 1968; Ciullo & Zarins, 1983; Grieve, 1970; Komi & Boscoe, 1978).

The only way to *increase power* is to *elongate the muscles' myofilaments past their current resting length prior to the sports activity.*

A muscle exerts its greatest tension when it functions at its greatest length. It can lift a greater load or produce a greater force the more it is pre-stretched from its resting length prior to contraction (Hill, A.V., 1956).

Chapter 5

BENEFITS OF STRETCHING

I. BENEFITS FOR ATHLETES: PERFORMANCE

By using proper warm-ups and stretches on a consistent basis, athletes can achieve their full potential in sports, *extend their best performance* for many years, and avoid the long-term consequences of secondary muscle, ligament, and joint damage caused by muscular imbalance and training errors.

Many young athletes have their personal-best performance when they are 16 or 17 years old. At this age they are still structurally immature.

At age 20-21 these athletes should be in their prime. They are more mature in the joint structure and have more *muscle mass.* Although this gives them more strength, they are unable to run as fast or jump as high as they could when they were younger. Many of these athletes are spending up to 50% of their training year trying to recover from chronic and recurring injuries, particularly to the knee, hip, and back.

These athletes have developed more *muscle mass and strength, but have less power.* They cannot equal their personal-best performance of earlier years and are chronically injured. This is a direct result of *too much strength and skill level training* combined with *not enough or incorrect stretches.*

With all strength-training programs it is essential to incorporate a stretching program. Get the strength by increasing the muscle mass through exercise, then get the power by elongating the individual muscle fibers through stretching.

II. BENEFITS FOR CHILDREN

Growing children are especially prone to developing muscle imbalances due to their rapid growth rate. Longitudinal growth occurs in the bones, along with the soft tissues such as the muscles and tendons. It is important that all children learn to stretch properly and consistently to maintain good muscle balance, joint range of motion, and to prevent injuries.

During periods of rapid growth there can be an increase in muscle-tendon tightness about the joints and a loss of range of motion due to the bones growing much faster than the muscles lengthen. (Kendall & Kendall, 1948; Leard, 1984; Micheli, 1983; Sutro, 1947).

III. BENEFITS FOR EVERYONE

It is important for people to realize how essential stretching is as ongoing maintenance of the weight-bearing muscles. Everyone needs to maintain good symmetry and length in these muscle groups in order to stay healthy and active.

A. Benefits of Maintaining Proper Muscle Length and Symmetry in the Lower Extremity

Muscle shortening will gradually change everyone's joint position and stride length. This in turn causes much of the chronic, insidious damage to the ligaments, which results in changes in joint position and posture.

Many people think that the chronic ache in their knees and lowback as they age is inevitable. "Rheumatism" is still a term often heard in discussions with elderly people.

Except for people with an underlying systemic disease such as rheumatoid arthritis, this is not true. Most of the chronic, low-level inflammation and pain in their muscles and joints is the result of *how they function, not how old they are.*

Most of these people can be helped by correcting the structural and muscle imbalances of their lower extremity through stretching. Better muscle function, joint position, and stride length will reduce the stress on their ligaments and joints.

No one has identified the problem and taught the older athlete how to change the muscle function that is causing the joint damage and postural changes (Corbin & Noble, 1980). Present medical treatment is all too often focused on the *symptom* instead of the *cause*.

Posture changes with aging because of ligament stretching and changes in joint position. This does not have to happen.

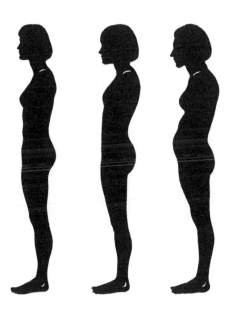

Postural Changes with Aging

B. Benefits from Relaxation of Muscle

Relaxation of the muscles is a valuable part of stretching. Excessive muscular tension tends to decrease sensory awareness and raise blood pressure (Larson & Michelman, 1973).

Habitually tense muscles tend to reduce their own circulation. Reduced blood supply results in a lack of oxygen and essential nutrients and causes toxic waste products to accumulate in the cells. *This will cause fatigue, aches, even pain.*

Relaxation is an economical energy consumption and resistance to fatigue (Basmajian, 1975). When more muscle fibers than necessary are activated, an inefficient energy expenditure results (Coville, 1979).

IV. PREVENTION OF INJURIES

When exercising to stimulate muscle growth (increase muscle mass), the length of the individual muscle fibers are shortened by the repetitive usage and fatigue. Over a prolonged period of time this muscle shortening can cause muscle imbalances that lead to ligament damage, joint hypermobility, and loss of function and power.

Stretching helps prevent injuries by not allowing the gradual, insidious shortening of the individual muscle fibers caused by repetitive usage and fatigue. The more the muscles are used, the more maintenance they require. *That maintenance is stretching.*

Chapter 6

SUMMARY

- Muscles are the contractile tissue that produce and control motion across the joints.

  - A sarcomere is the individual muscle fiber containing two myofilaments.

- The myofilaments contain the actin and myosin protein fibers. It is the actin and myosin protein fibers sliding back and forth past each other that expend energy and produce motion. *The myofilaments are the contractile tissues of the muscle that produce contractions.*

  - A myofilament has a resting length, where the muscle is not expending energy or doing work.

SUMMARY

- A myofilament has a maximum contraction, where the protein overlap cannot shorten any further. The myofilament length cannot shorten past that point.

  - *All movement and exercise* takes place somewhere between a muscle's *current resting length* and it's *maximum contraction.*

- *STRENGTH* is defined as contractibility, the capacity to shorten and the ability to develop tension. Exercise increases the number of individual muscle fibers (myofilaments), increasing the muscle mass. The larger the muscle mass, the more tension the muscle can develop.

  - *POWER* is defined as how much load a muscle can move and how fast that muscle can move a specific load. Power comes from the longest length of contraction possible in the *individual muscle fibers.*

- The only way to elongate the muscle fibers past the current resting length and gain more power is *through proper stretches.*

  - A stretch is a sliding elongation of the overlapping protein fibers of the myofilaments *past their current resting length.* This results in an elongation of the myofilaments.

- *ENERGY* is stored in the muscle during this sliding elongation, giving the muscle more *POWER.*

SUMMARY

- The non-weight-bearing muscles of the arms will have approximately the same resting length throughout a lifetime. They simply are not functioning under the constant and enormous load of the weight-bearing muscles of the lower extremity.

- The weight-bearing muscles of the lower extremity will slowly shorten in their resting length over the years with repetitive usage, even without sports involvement. The *current resting length* is very seldom the *best resting length* in these muscles.

- These muscles will remain shortened and asymmetrical if the person does not learn the importance of stretching, and how to do proper stretches.

- In athletes, this gradual shortening will affect their performance levels as well as lead to chronic injuries.

- In everyone, the shortening of the lower extremity muscles will lead to changes in joint position and stride length in all walking functions. This will always lead to gradual ligament damage, causing changes in joint position and posture.

- Stretching of the weight-bearing muscle groups of the lower extremity is the *body maintenance* that we need throughout life. With proper stretching we can achieve better function and more power; and avoid many of the long-term problems such as arthritis, muscle stiffness and chronic discomfort that affect so many people.

NOTES

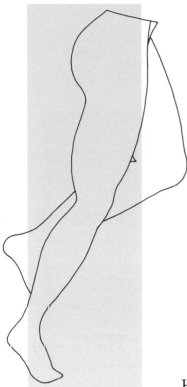

SECTION 2

Muscle Preparation

How to Stretch

Mistakes in Stretching

Having discussed muscle anatomy and the mechanisms of the muscle myofilament elongation during a "stretch," we now need to know how to make this knowledge practical for everyone. Before the proper stretch for each of the weight-bearing muscle groups is described, several related topics must be examined.

Chapter 7   Preparing to Stretch, Proper Warm-up Exercises

Chapter 8   Primary Stretches and Skill-level Stretches

Chapter 9   How to Stretch

Chapter 10   Five Golden Rules of Stretching

Chapter 11   Mistakes In Stretching

Chapter 12   Different Stretching Theories

Chapter 7

Preparing to Stretch: Proper Warm-up Exercises

The terms warm-ups and stretches are often confused. Warm-up exercises are not stretches. In order to prevent injury to the muscles it is important to do warm-up exercises as a *preparation* for stretches.

I. Definition

Warm-ups are not stretches. Warm-ups are *gentle exercises* done to prepare the muscles for stretching.

- Cold muscle has a poor blood supply, a high viscosity (meaning it has a high chemical *inelasticity*), and therefore can be easily injured by stretching without doing proper warm-up exercises first.

■ Warm-up exercises are defined as repetitive contractions of the muscles under a light to moderate load, in order to literally increase the heat (warmth, blood flow) of the muscles. During these repetitive gentle contractions the blood flow increases, and the viscosity of the muscle decreases (the elasticity of the muscle increases).

Stretches should always be *preceded* by a mild set of warm-up exercises. The increase in the tissue temperature and blood flow produced by the muscular exercise will make the stretching both safer and more productive (Sapega et al., 1981).

II. TYPES OF WARM-UPS

A. Walking

A classic example of a gentle, repetitive contraction is walking. WALKING is an ideal warm-up exercise. A five-minute walk is a good warm-up. A ten-minute walk is an exemplary warm-up. While walking the muscles of the upper and lower extremities, especially the five major weight-bearing muscle groups of the lower extremity, are going through repetitive gentle contractions. These repetitive contractions under a light load increase the blood flow and elasticity of the muscles. It is important to understand that the *weight-bearing impact* of walking is *three to four times less* than running or jumping.

B. Gentle Power Movements with Light Weights

Using light weights in weight training has been recommended as warm-up exercises for specific muscle groups in some research.

The purpose of warming up is to raise the internal temperature and reduce the viscosity in the muscles. The Russians have found that preliminary strength-training exercises for the hamstring muscles in warm-ups prevents rupture of the muscle fibers.

Volkov and Mironova studied the temperature of the thigh (femoral) muscles and observed a *decrease* in the temperature of these muscles during common but incorrect warm-up exercises. After inclusion of power exercises for the hamstrings at the beginning of the warm-up, an increase of 1.6 to 2.6 degrees (centigrade) was recorded in the muscles internal temperature (Volkov, M.V. & Mironova, Z.S., 1966).

C. Other Warm-up Exercises

Other exercises such as cycling, treadmill, and rowing at moderate loads are also good warm-up exercises.

III. INCORRECT WARM-UPS

There are many examples of incorrect warm-up exercises, including *running slowly* and *jumping rope,* which often lead to injury.

To understand why running slowly to warm up is a training error, we need to understand how the body absorbs the shock of the landing impact through muscle function; and how the body spreads (*dissipates*) that shock over the largest surface area of the joints. There are three important factors involved in the *mechanisms of shock absorption* and the *dissipation of that shock* in walking and running.

IV. MECHANISMS OF SHOCK ABSORPTION

A. Muscle Function

B. Joint Range of Motion

C. Horizontal Displacement of the Body Mass

A. Muscle Function

The lower-extremity muscles, elongating and shortening in stride (eccentric and concentric muscle contractures), absorb most of the shock of the landing impact. Muscle function is the number-one *"shock absorber"* of the body.

Description of Shock Absorption by the Lower Leg Muscles:

The lower leg muscles, whose tendons extend into the foot, absorb shock. These muscle groups must elongate and expend energy (an eccentric contraction) to decelerate the forefoot impact and absorb shock all the way through pronation (the first stage of the midstance phase of gait in everyone).

Cold muscles cannot elongate under load (eccentrically contract) effectively, because the muscles do not have good blood flow or elasticity. The sudden ballistic loading of the landing impact causes thousands of microtears at the muscle-tendon junctions of both the anterior and deep posterior muscle groups of the lower leg.

SHOCK ABSORPTION

- This chronic tearing of tissue causes the pain and pressure from swelling (edema) in *shin splints*.

- If enough tissue is torn to have serious swelling and increased pressure in the surrounding fascial compartment, it is referred to as a *compartment syndrome*.

- Because these muscles are not absorbing shock and the bone is trying to reorganize and increase its calcium density to handle the increased shock, this often results in a *tibial* or *metatarsal stress fracture*.

One of the most common causes of shin splints, compartment syndromes and stress fractures is a very simple training error: *running slowly to warm up*. By the time the athlete is clinically symptomatic, the microscopic tearing has been occurring for a prolonged period of time.

B. Joint Range of Motion

The next important component of the body's ability to handle the shock of the landing impact is joint range of motion. The longer the stride, the larger the range of motion (of the foot, ankle, knee, and hip joints). This spreads the shock over the largest articular surface area of each joint. There is *less impact* on any given part of the cartilage of each joint. Spreading the landing impact over a larger area of the articular cartilage of the joint diminishes the shock on that joint.

C. Horizontal Displacement of the Body Mass

The more horizontal momentum of the body mass, parallel to the ground, the *less vertical vector force* into the ground. In other words, the better the horizontal momentum, the less impact when the foot strikes the ground (see example next page).

SHOCK ABSORPTION

Example:

The following example demonstrates how these three factors affect shock absorption.

A 200-lb. man walking at a steady pace with good muscle function, joint position, and stride length, will hit the ground with his body weight plus approximately 20% (which amounts to about *240 lb./ sq. in. of loading force* as his foot impacts on the ground).

The same 200 lb. man running well, not sprinting *but not jogging slowly*, has almost the identical muscle function and joint range of motion as he had walking, but with a longer stride length. He maintains good horizontal momentum of his body mass but *significantly increases his velocity,* which will triple the weight-bearing impact into the ground. The *momentum of impact* is now approximately *720 lb./ sq. in.* while running at a decent stride length, and *he is still maximizing the body's ability to absorb and dissipate that shock.*

Jogging slowly shortens the stride, *reducing the joint range of motion* and *decreasing muscle function.* The body's ability to absorb and dissipate shock has been decreased. The slow runner also loses or greatly reduces the horizontal momentum, therefore *the*

SHOCK ABSORPTION

vertical vector force is increased. He has reduced his body's ability to handle impact and at the same time has increased the amount of weight-bearing impact it has to handle. Running slowly, he has a *400% increase* over the weight-bearing impact of walking, and strikes the ground with about *960 lb./sq. in.*

V. SUMMARY

By studying the physics of the landing impact, it is obvious that running slowly has a higher landing impact than when running at a faster pace. When running slowly the body has less ability to absorb and dissipate that shock, especially if the lower leg muscles are cold. Running slowly to warm up is a training error.

Because of the increased joint trauma, running slowly over long periods of time on hard surfaces will create degenerative changes of the knee, pelvis, and spine in anyone, regardless of age, gender, or athletic ability.

Chapter 8

PRIMARY STRETCHES AND SKILL-LEVEL STRETCHES

There are two levels of stretches. Everyone needs to do primary stretches for health and well-being. Only athletes, who are doing movements that require an extremely large range of motion across their joints, should be doing skill-level stretches.

I. PRIMARY STRETCHES

Primary stretches isolate one major muscle or muscle group across one joint, in a position where the muscle group can relax back to its resting length and slide longer. Structures such as the ligaments of the joints or the joint capsules are not loaded if the stretch is done with proper positioning. Important structures like the sciatic nerve in the posterior pelvis are not put under any traction which could result in damage.

Isolates the
Hamstring Muscles

No Load on Pelvic
or Spinal Ligaments

II. SKILL-LEVEL STRETCHES

Skill-level stretches load more than one major muscle group, and place a heavy load on other structures of the body, especially the ligaments of the pelvis and spine. They should only be done *after* the individual muscle groups have stretched to their maximum length in a primary stretch, and only after years of training beginning at an early age.

The ligaments of the body have the most elasticity during early puberty and adolescence. Growth harmones allow ligaments to elongate without tearing in order to keep up with the rapid growth of the bones. If the ligament elongation was not able to keep pace with the rapid growth of the bones at this age, everyone would suffer some ligament tearing and damage. Stretches that place a large load on the ligaments must be learned at this time of life, and continued through the adult years.

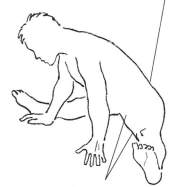

Loading Pelvic and
Lumbar Ligaments

Loading Adductor and
Medial Hamstring Muscles

Because the growth hormone is no longer present in adults, anyone trying to start these skill-level stretches as adults will suffer tearing and damage to the ligaments.

Chapter 9

How to Stretch

After careful consideration of the published literature of the last sixty years, and my experiences both as an amateur and professional athlete, followed by years as a physician specializing in sports medicine, I have come to this conclusion:

For the majority of people, whether active athletes or those trying to stay healthy, stretching is of vital importance. In order to accomplish their stretches and not cause damage to the muscles or other structures, certain criteria must be met in terms of positioning and which specific structures are loaded. The following are the criteria for proper static stretches.

1. The stretch must be simple and can be accomplished by *one individual* without the aid of a partner.

2. The stretch must isolate *one major muscle* or muscle group of the lower extremity in a position where that muscle group can relax back to its resting length and slide longer.

3. With proper positioning and isolation of one specific muscle group other structures such as ligaments and the sciatic nerve are not loaded to any significant level.

4. When stretching before any athletic activity, I recommend that each muscle group be stretched twice in succession. The way to accomplish this is to find the first tension and wait for that tension to release, then find that same gentle tension a second time and allow the muscle to elongate again.

DISCUSSION

Discussion of Criteria 4:

■ When the muscle group is loaded gently, the muscle fibers relax back to their current resting length fairly quickly, and the sliding elongation then occurs. This is experienced as a loss of sensation (tension).

  ■ Because the muscles are being loaded gently, there is not enough tension to cause the muscle fibers to slide a great distance. Once the first tension is gone, find that gentle tension again; and allow the second loss of sensation (tension).

■ The muscle fibers are now *two segments longer* in their myofilaments than before the initial stretch.

  ■ Sometimes it is possible to do three segments of stretching on a muscle group, although often the tension you feel in the third segment does not decrease. This is because the myofilaments have reached their longest possible length. The actin protein cannot slide past the last cross-link with the myosin protein, or the myofilament would tear.

You now have the most power from the longest length of contraction possible!

Breathing enhances stretching:

Controlled breathing not only facilitates relaxation, it also enhances stretching (Jencks, 1977). Stretching is enhanced by exhalation. Inhaling slowly and deeply, followed by exhaling slowly and completely, will facilitate the muscles' relaxation and elongation past their current resting length.

Chapter 10

THE 5 GOLDEN RULES OF STRETCHING

The five rules of stretching are stated below. These rules apply to any major muscle group, and incorporate the information contained in the previous chapters. By following these simple guidelines many benefits are gained, including better symmetry, length, and power in your muscles.

Isolate the Muscle Group

- Isolate the muscle group across one joint in a position where the muscle group is not expending energy to maintain position.
- The positioning of the muscle group should not load other structures such as ligaments or joint capsules.

Find Zero Tension

- Zero tension is when there is *no awareness of tension* in a muscle group because there is no load and resulting tension on that muscle group.
- When you start with *no tension* in the muscle group and then find the first tension or awareness, the biofeedback of that muscle group is more subtle and accurate.
- When you start a stretch with tension in the muscle group and try to adjust the tension on that muscle group, the biofeedback is not as subtle or accurate.

Find the First Awareness

- Find the first gentle tension in the muscle group *(the gentle reflex contraction against the loading force)*. This is the first awareness of a stretch.
- Loading the muscles harder serves no purpose! It will take longer for the muscles to relax back to their original resting length. The sliding elongation of the overlapping protein fibers past the original resting length *does not start* until that relaxation has occurred.
- By loading the muscles harder the desired effect is delayed and there is more risk of injury due to overstretching.
- This leads us to Rule #4.

Less is Best

- As explained above, the more gentle the initial load on a muscle or muscle group in a stretch, the faster the muscle group can relax back to the current resting length.
- The muscle group must relax back to the *current resting length* before the sliding elongation past the resting length can begin.

Allow the Loss of Tension

- Stretches *cannot* be timed. The gentle tension must be steady and constant on the muscle if the muscle fibers are going to relax and slide past their current resting length.
- The duration of a stretch changes daily. It is determined by many factors:
  - The amount of initial load on the muscle group.
  - The amount of warm-up before the stretch.
  - The fatigue in the muscle, or any inflammation from injury or overuse.
- Find the first gentle tension in the muscle group and maintain a steady position until the tension is gone.
- *Allow* the muscles the time required for the relaxation/elongation. *You cannot make it happen.* Do not watch the clock. Listen to your body and depend on your biofeedback.

BIOFEEDBACK

Biofeedback is the body awareness *developed* through movement, exercise, and stretches. Most people have been taught to stretch with intensity or pain in the muscles ("No Pain, No Gain" has been the maxim). Their biofeedback has been conditioned to intensity.

Initially these people may have trouble feeling the gentle tension of a proper stretch. This will change with proper stretching techniques and practice. Learning to find the first gentle tension in the muscles will result in better and more subtle biofeedback.

Chapter 11

MISTAKES IN STRETCHING

Many young athletes and people in fitness programs are causing themselves long-term damage because of training errors instead of benefiting from their participation.

Older athletes are far more crippled by the *muscle imbalances, ligament weakening, joint hypermobility,* and the *resulting joint damage* caused by these training errors over a lifetime than by all of the acute injuries they have experienced.

Common mistakes in stretching are due to:

- Timing
- Positioning errors
- Loading other structures
- Overstretching

I. TIMING

Timing relates to two aspects of stretching:

A. How long to hold any one stretch

People are taught that a stretch can be timed. "Hold that stretch for thirty seconds" is a common recommendation. This is *incorrect. No one can time stretches.*

When loading a muscle, the relaxation time back to the original resting length will vary greatly from individual to individual.

It will also vary in the same person from day to day because of fatigue and lactic acid. A tired muscle is full of lactic acid and is shorter and chemically more inelastic. It will have a much longer relaxation time than the same muscle the day it is rested.

The timing of a stretch is determined by holding the position until the tension in the muscle group is gone.

B. When to stretch
(the time lapse between the stretch and the competition)

A stretch should *immediately precede* the skill-level activity or sports competition in order for the athlete to take advantage of the increased power of the muscles. If a sprinter warms up and stretches, then stands around for 20-30 minutes before the competition, the muscles will contract back to their original resting length. *As a result, the energy stored in the muscles by stretching is WASTED.*

If a muscle is not used after stretching, relaxation back toward its current resting length will occur. The energy stored in the stretching is not taken advantage of and the stored elastic energy is dissipated as heat (Hill, 1961).

II. POSITIONING

The muscle or muscle group must be isolated in a position *where the muscles are not contracted or expending energy* to maintain a position or posture.

There are many examples of incorrect stretching positions where the muscle group is *involuntarily contracted* to stabilize the body against gravity. All standing hamstring muscle stretches are an example of this positioning error. These are described in detail in Section 3.

III. LOADING OTHER STRUCTURES

Primary stretches isolate one muscle group across one joint, without loading other structures unrelated or connected to this specific muscle group or joint.

There are many examples of loading other structures and the damage that can occur to ligaments, joint capsules, and the sciatic nerve as a result. These will be discussed in detail as each muscle group is described in Section 3. Here, ligaments are used as an example.

When a ligament is put under a continuous and protracted stress it will gradually elongate.

As described in the section on the different properties of connective tissue, ligaments in adults can only elongate through a process of *microscopic tearing, scarring, and weakening*. This is call *plastic deformity.*

The weakened and elongated ligaments are no longer able to stabilize the bones of the joint properly, which results in hypermobility of the joint. This excessive joint motion causes joint trauma and chronic inflammation. The chronic inflammation results in the gradual destruction of the joint cartilage. This destruction of the joint cartilage is called degenerative arthritis (osteoarthritis).

Any stretch that loads the joints and places an abnormal stress on the ligaments will slowly cause permanent damage to the ligaments. The so-called "hurdler's stretch" is a classic example. In stretching the hamstrings of one leg, the ligaments of the opposite knee are placed under abnormal stress.

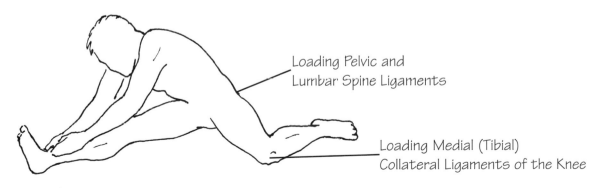

Loading Pelvic and Lumbar Spine Ligaments

Loading Medial (Tibial) Collateral Ligaments of the Knee

When the knee is flexed and externally rotated in this *weight-bearing* position there is an abnormal load placed on the medial collateral ligaments of the knee. Flexion of the knee joint in this position will damage the ligaments (Rapoport, 1984; Anderson, 1980).

When this is done repetitively over a long period of time, the end result is the tearing, scarring, and weakening of the ligaments of the bent knee, as the athlete tries to stretch the hamstrings of the other leg.

IV. OVERSTRETCHING

Overstretching is placing too much tension on a muscle group, causing damage to the muscle fibers.

Overstretching causes microscopic tearing at the muscle-tendon junctions, the weakest part of any muscle, and causes permanent scarring (fibrosis) in the muscle fibers. With a major overload, the tendon attachment to the bone can be torn, especially in children. *Remember, the tendon fibers cannot elongate more than 3-4% without rupturing the tendon.*

The problem with overstretching is that it does not hurt during the stretch. People feel the contraction and pull in the wrong place, but don't feel pain. The resulting microscopic tearing is not sufficient to cause *immediate* inflammation in the structures. The *minor soreness* at the ends of the muscles is usually more apparent the *next day*.

Knowing where to feel the tension during a stretch, **AND WHERE NOT TO FEEL ANY TENSION**, is very important. When viewing the illustrations of each muscle group in Section 3 this is easily understood.

Examples:

- You should never feel any tension up to or behind the knee when doing calf stretches. The upper muscle-tendon junction of the gastrocnemius muscle is just below the knee joint. There is very little gastrocnemius muscle behind the knee, only *joint capsule* and the gastrocnemius muscle's tendon of origin.

- You should not feel any tension from a hand's width above the knee down to the knee when doing hamstring stretches. The hamstring's muscle-tendon junction is 4-8 inches above the knee. When the tension of the stretch is felt behind the knee, there is no immediate sensation of pain.

- When the muscle is crampy and sore at the ends of the muscles (tendon junctions) *the next day*, you don't realize that the stretch the day before has caused the damage.

V. GOOD SORENESS/BAD SORENESS

How do you know when you are making mistakes while stretching? The microscopic tearing caused by overstretching does not cause immediate inflammation and pain. It often takes 12-24 hours for the inflammation and minor discomfort caused by that tearing to become obvious.

Because you usually do not register pain when overstretching, you need to become aware of the body's signals *the next day.* Body awareness the next day will help you to learn the difference between good soreness and bad soreness.

A. Good Soreness

When muscles are exercised to fatigue (anaerobic metabolism), they will be sore and stiff *throughout the entire muscle* the next morning. After hours of movement, with increased blood flow and lymphatic drainage, this morning soreness gradually disappears.

This is the *good soreness* of endurance or strength training. The explanation for this soreness is varied in the literature.

GOOD SORENESS

The accumulation of lactic acid, the excessive accumulation of metabolites that cause an increased osmotic pressure inside and outside muscle fiber, retained excess water causing edema and pressure on sensory nerves are just a few of the current theories (Asmussen, 1956; Karpovich & Sinning, 1971).

Others feel that the swelling of the muscle tissue with the accumulation of metabolites causes the muscle to become shorter, thicker, and more resistant to stretching or movement. This is what causes the sensation of stiffness (Morehouse & Miller, 1971).

The old and inaccurate theory that muscle soreness is due to microscopic tearing of the muscle fibers and connective tissue (Hough, 1902) is incorrect. It is not sensible or plausible to think that a tissue is structurally damaged by the function for which it is specifically differentiated (de Vries, 1961a, 1961b, 1962, 1966).

B. Bad Soreness

If the good soreness goes away, and there is pain or obvious discomfort at the end of the muscle, or in the ligaments or joint capsules, this is the *bad soreness caused by training errors.*

This bad soreness of microscopic tearing and scarring can last for days or weeks; and in some cases last the entire training year.

It is imperative to teach people simple landmarks of muscle anatomy, and to teach the difference between good soreness and bad soreness.

Summary:

By learning simple landmarks of the body and understanding the concept of *good soreness/bad soreness,* you can recognize and eliminate training errors and the resulting injuries.

Chapter 12

STRETCHING TECHNIQUES

There has been a lot of research concerning how muscles function, and what is the best method of stretching. Everyone in sports seems to have a different theory on this topic. The following is a brief review of some of these stretching techniques. When studied closely, some of the stretching techniques do not make sense when the mechanisms of stretching are understood. Other techniques, like PNF stretching, require a thorough knowledge of neuromuscular function and a well-trained partner.

I. DYNAMIC STRETCHES

Dynamic stretches, also called active extensions, are not stretches *by definition*. The muscles are isometrically contracting to maintain the position. As previously discussed, *this is not a stretch* because the muscles cannot relax back to their current resting length; therefore no sliding elongation past the current resting length can occur.

A classic example of a dynamic contraction is the runner's "stretch."

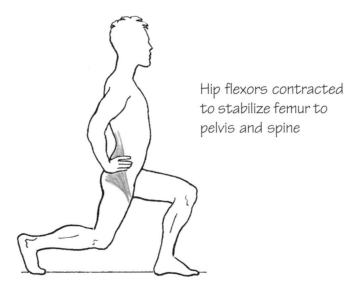

Hip flexors contracted to stabilize femur to pelvis and spine

Although dynamic extensions are not stretches, they are *good mobilization exercises*, and will help maintain healthy sarcomeres at the ends of the muscles.

Muscles that have been shortened by injury or lack of use lose the sarcomeres at the ends of the muscle. One study showed a 40% loss of sarcomeres in series with prolonged contracture (Tabary et al., 1972).

Muscles that are *continually placed in an extended position* can regenerate sarcomeres in series at the ends of the muscle. This is why dynamic extensions and end of range of motion exercises are beneficial. There should never be any ballistic or bouncing motions to these mobilization exercises.

II. PNF STRETCHES

One of the most often discussed forms of stretching is the PNF method. PNF stands for *Proprioceptive Neuromuscular Facilitation*. How many people can pronounce this, much less know what it means or how to accomplish it effectively without causing damage?

Two people are required for most PNF stretches. The technique requires the person stretching to contract the muscle group being stretched against resistance from the partner. Then the *opposite muscle group is contracted* while tension to the muscle group being stretched is applied by the partner. The opposite muscle group must remain consciously contracted while tension is maintained on the muscles being stretched.

There are a number of things that can cause injury with this method. Too much tension can be applied to the muscles by the partner, the stretcher can lose concentration and stop contracting the opposite muscle group, or *overzealous athletes can turn something subtle into a contest.* This method is for PNF-trained professionals only.

A trained assistant with good anatomical and *neuromuscular knowledge* is an absolute necessity for proper PNF stretching. This is the main reason for most athletes to avoid these types of stretches. Fellow athletes, the coach, even the team trainer can not be expected to be fully aware of all the parameters for these functions without extensive education in this specific area of expertise.

PNF STRETCHES

PNF stretches are designed as partner stretches, and if done incorrectly can cause injury (Beaulieu, 1981; Cornelius, 1983).

PNF stretches can be more dangerous than static stretching because more tension is placed on the muscle. With excessive tension on the muscle, the stretch must be monitored closely to reduce the incidence of soft-tissue injury.

PNF techniques have potential benefits, but they also have the potential for damage and negative results. PNF methods can be uncomfortable or even painful, and they require a very motivated person (Moore & Hutton, 1980; Cornelius, 1983).

In addition, experiments have challenged some of the ideas supporting the neurophysiological basis of PNF stretching (Eldred, Hutton, & Smith, 1976; Suzuki & Hutton, 1976).

III. Passive-active and Active-assisted Stretches

Both of these types of so-called stretches employ some "dynamic" movement and some PNF function. They are more difficult and require specifically trained assistance.

In passive stretching the motion or load is performed by an outside agent responsible for the stretch. A partner or special equipment is necessary.

IV. Static Stretches

Static stretches are accomplished by loading the muscles and allowing the relaxation and sliding elongation described in the *mechanisms of stretching*. *No assistance or special equipment* is needed, and the stretches can be done anywhere. This is the type of stretch described in the following chapters for each specific weight-bearing muscle group.

STATIC STRETCHES

Research has demonstrated that permanent lengthening is most favored by *lower force, longer duration stretching* at elevated temperatures (Laban, 1962; Light, Nuzik, Personius, & Barstrom, 1984; Warren, Lehmann, & Koblanski, 1971, 1976).

Static stretching is preferable because it requires less energy expenditure than other methods, it results in less muscle soreness, and it can provide more qualitative relief from muscle soreness (de Vries, 1966, 1980).

It is the best method of stretching for the individual.

The following stretches are the best *primary* stretches for the six weight-bearing muscle groups of the lower extremity. They are the best stretches found that follow all the rules of proper static stretching.

NOTES

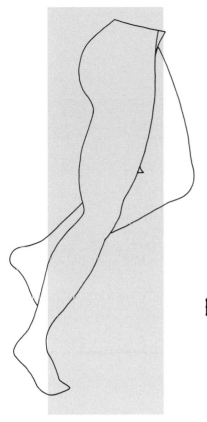

SECTION 3

PRIMARY STRETCHES
FOR THE MAJOR WEIGHT-BEARING
MUSCLE GROUPS OF THE
LOWER EXTREMITY

In this section the primary stretches for each of the major muscle groups of the lower extremity will be described. If a primary stretch of any muscle group can be done in more than one position, we have included these other positions.

The other stretching positions illustrated and discussed all present problems and can cause injury. Some of the improper stretches illustrated are skill-level stretches, loading more than one major muscle group across the same joint, while placing a heavy load on ligament structures. Others are incorrect because of positioning; the muscles cannot relax back to their resting length if they are contracted, expending energy, to hold a position.

The first two sections of this book explained the structures involved and how they function; this section will help you apply that knowledge to gain the most from your stretches and avoid the long-term damage created by doing them incorrectly.

Chapter 13   Calf Muscles (Gastrocnemius and Soleus)

Chapter 14   Groin Muscles (Adductors)

Chapter 15   Quadriceps

Chapter 16   Hamstrings

Chapter 17   Posterior Hip Muscles (Gluteal muscles and External Hip Rotators)

Chapter 18   Hip Flexors (Psoas and Iliacus)

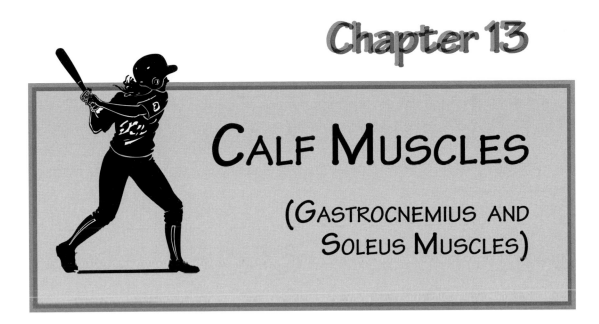

CHAPTER 13

CALF MUSCLES

(GASTROCNEMIUS AND SOLEUS MUSCLES)

The gastrocnemius and soleus muscles are collectively known as the calf muscles. The gastrocnemius is the more posterior muscle and forms the greater part of the calf.

The soleus is a broad, flat muscle situated immediately underneath (anterior to) the gastrocnemius. The tendons of the gastrocnemius and soleus form the achilles tendon (tendo calcancus).

The achilles tendon is one of the largest tendons in the body. It is attached to the posterior surface of the heel bone (calcaneus). The tendon is extremely strong and inelastic, but is vulnerable to injury.

We will discuss the two muscles separately. It is important to note that the gastrocnemius muscle crosses both the knee and ankle joint, while the soleus only crosses the ankle joint.

I. GASTROCNEMIUS MUSCLE

A. Anatomy

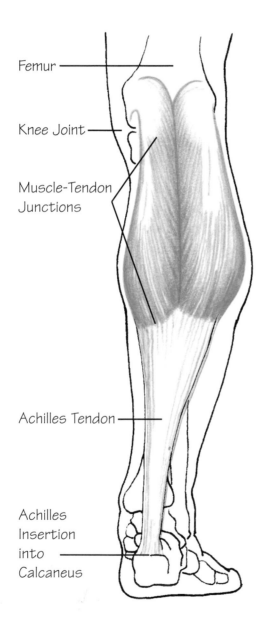

Femur

Knee Joint

Muscle-Tendon
Junctions

Achilles Tendon

Achilles
Insertion
into
Calcaneus

The gastrocnemius has two tendons of origin that are attached to the back of the thigh bone (the femoral condyles) above the knee joint. The tendons of origin cross the back of the knee joint, and the muscle-tendon junctions are slightly below the knee joint.

The gastrocnemius has a large, round, fairly short muscle belly whose definition is easily seen in most people. The lower muscle-tendon junction is the starting point of the achilles tendon, which is the tendon of insertion.

The achilles tendon crosses the ankle joint and is attached to the heel bone (calcaneus).

B. Biomechanics

The gastrocnemius is one of the most important muscles in the body. When you are walking or running, the *eccentric capacity of the gastrocnemius muscle* determines your *joint position* and *stride length*. To understand how this works, the *eccentric function* of this muscle during the *midstance phase* of the *normal gait cycle* must be understood.

C. Normal Gait Cycle

The normal gait cycle consists of four phases:

1. Swing phase of gait - when the leg is moving through the air.

2. Heel contact - the swing phase of gait ends when the heel contacts the ground. The heel-contact phase lasts until the forefoot reaches the ground.

3. Midstance phase of gait - the midstance phase begins when the lateral aspect of the forefoot contacts the ground and lasts until the heel is lifted off the ground. It is during this phase of gait, when the entire foot is on the ground, that *pronation* followed by *resupination* of the foot should occur. Both pronation and resupination are necessary segments of foot motion in the midstance phase of gait for shock absorption and joint repositioning *before* the heel is lifted off the ground.

4. Propulsive phase of gait - this phase lasts from heel lift until the ball of the foot leaves the ground.

II. MIDSTANCE PHASE OF THE NORMAL GAIT CYCLE

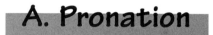

A. Pronation

In the midstance phase of gait, the forefoot hits the ground, the leg is moving forward over the foot, and the gastrocnemius is contracting eccentrically. This means the gastrocnemius is elongating, expending energy and doing work: keeping the knee flexed to prevent hyperextension of the knee.

As the foot hits the ground it *pronates* (meaning the arch height decreases and the foot lengthens under the weight-bearing impact). Pronation allows the lower leg muscles, whose tendons cross the ankle joint into the foot, to continue to absorb shock through their elongating (*eccentric*) contractions. *Pronation is a normal and necessary part of every stride.* Pronation allows the joint motion necessary for the lower leg muscles to function fully and absorb shock.

At the end of the pronation phase there is a heavy load on the ligament structures of the pronated foot. The knee is now internally rotated with increased angulation of the patella tendon containing the knee cap, and there is increased stress on the medial knee ligaments. The femur is rotated inward (medially), causing increased load on the hip flexors and external hip rotator muscles, as well as the ligaments of the sacroiliac joints of the pelvis.

B. Resupination

As the leg continues forward over the foot, which is fixed on the ground, the lower leg muscles start to shorten (concentrically contract) at the end of the pronation phase and lift the bony arch of the foot. This is called *resupination*.

> During resupination, the arch height starts to increase and the foot shortens slightly. During resupination the knee externally rotates and realigns the patella mechanism and decreases the load on the ligaments of the knee. The femur, hip, and pelvis also attain better alignment.

The gastrocnemius muscle is *still eccentrically contracting*, keeping the knee slightly flexed. When the lower leg's forward movement causes the gastrocnemium muscle fibers to slightly exceed their *eccentric capacity*, the overlapping proteins in the myofilaments are extended *past their current resting length*. The muscle spindles react by *myotatic reflex contraction* to keep the muscles from being torn.

> This lower motor neuron reflex contraction results in an almost *isometric* contraction of the gastrocnemius muscle. The gastrocnemius is expending energy and resisting further elongation. This isometric contraction (expending energy but not changing length) of the gastrocnemius muscle lifts the heel off the ground because the leg is continuing forward over the foot, but the gastrocnemius has stopped elongating.

RESUPINATION

This is how the *current resting length* and *eccentric capacity* of the gastrocnemius muscle determines your *joint position* and *stride length*. There must be enough eccentric capacity in the gastrocnemius muscle to allow the lower extremity to complete the full gait cycle.

Pronation followed by resupination are normal segments of the gait cycle. These movements are necessary for proper function of the joints and shock absorption by the muscles of the lower extremity. This also allows proper positioning of the foot, knee, hip, and pelvis.

III. STRUCTURAL DAMAGE CAUSED BY SHORTENED CALF MUSCLES

The calf muscles, especially the gastrocnemius muscle, are always *the first muscles to shorten with repetitive usage and fatigue*. This shortening of the current resting length in the calf muscle reduces the muscle's eccentric capacity. This loss of eccentric capacity results in a short stride with poor joint position. Without proper stretches, these muscles will remain shortened for the rest of your life.

A. Stress on the Ligaments of the Lower Extremity

Proper joint position and stride length are not possible with a *shortened gastrocnemius muscle*. The reflex response of the gastrocnemius muscle lifts the heel prematurely, while the foot is still pronated. The resupination phase of gait does not occur because of this premature lifting of the heel off the ground by the calf muscles. The pronated foot is not the problem; the calf muscle *lifting the heel while the foot is still pronated* is the problem.

The heel lifting while the foot is still pronated causes abnormal stress on the ligament structures of the arch of the foot, especially the large structure known as the *plantar fascia.*

It also causes the heel to lift with the knee still internally rotated, because resupination of the foot and the realignment of the knee have not occurred. This results in stress to the ligaments of the knee joint, and excessive pull and angulation of the quadriceps muscles and tendon (patella tendon) where it attaches to the leg bone (tibia) below the knee.

Osgood-Schlatter disease, patella-femoral syndrome, and chondromalacia are terms used to describe the pain and inflammation of this damage. These medical terms describe what has been damaged, *what hurts.*

This excessive stress, with a resulting accumulation of microtrauma and secondary inflammation, is a leading cause of knee damage in young athletes; and *in every-one* as we get older.

When a patient has these types of symptoms, the treatment should focus on the *structural and muscular imbalances* that are causing the damage. The treatment should be focused on the *cause* instead of the symptoms.

Many health professionals are treating the *symptoms* instead of the cause.

B. Bunions

All bunions are caused by the short stride and the abductory twist off the big-toe joint (first metatarsal-phalangeal joint) in the propulsive phase of gait caused by the shortened gastrocnemius muscles. When heel lift occurs before you have finished the swing phase of the opposite leg, you spin off the weight-bearing foot in order to gain the time needed to get the opposite leg in front of the pelvis.

- Bunions are a growing bone deformity (bone spur) with ligament stretching and secondary joint dislocation, resulting in degenerative arthritis (osteoarthritis).
- The constant pressure on the side of the first metatarsal at the joint causes the bone to hypertrophy (the bone continues to enlarge to protect itself), which causes the bone spur (exostosis).
- The constant stress on the medial ligaments of the big-toe joint (first metatarsal-phalangeal joint) causes microscopic tearing, weakening, and lengthening. This results in the gradual lateral dislocation of the joint.
- The chronic-loading stress and inflammation in the joint will lead to destruction of the articular cartilage (osteoarthritis) over a period of time.
- Other factors such as the shape of the big-toe joint, the elasticity of your ligament structures (an inherited characteristic), and the shoes you wear affect how fast a bunion will form. But without the tight calf muscles and the spinning rotation off the side of the big-toe joint in the propulsive phase of gait, no bunion will form.

BUNIONS

Example:

Walk or run behind your friends and observe which heel lifts the fastest, and how they twist in at the heel as they spin off the inside of that forefoot. The leg with the earliest heel lift and the most abductory twist of the foot will have the larger bunion.

Eliminating the tight calf muscles, by doing proper gastrocnemius muscle stretches, will re-establish good joint position and stride length, and will hinder further development of bunions.

C. Asymmetry

Everyone has a dominant side in terms of muscle coordination and reflex response to loading force. You are either right-handed or left-handed, meaning right or left dominance in neuromuscular control.

The reflex response to loading force is slightly faster on the dominant side. This causes muscles to function slightly quicker, fatigue faster, and shorten more on the dominant side. This results in many people being asymmetrical in their joint position and stride length when walking or running. The resulting asymmetry in the muscles can even be seen when a person is standing still.

Example:

ASYMMETRY

Many people stand with one foot and leg turned out (externally rotated) much more than the other. This asymmetry in their stance results from the gluteal muscles and the external hip rotator muscles of the posterior pelvis being tighter, which externally rotates the femur, turning that leg out more.

For proper
joint position and stride length,
the most important stretch
for everyone
throughout life is the

GASTROCNEMIUS MUSCLE STRETCH.

IV. GASTROCNEMIUS STRETCH: BOTH LEGS AT THE SAME TIME

Isolate the Muscle Group

- To isolate the gastrocnemius muscles the best position is standing with the entire ball of both feet resting on a raised surface and the heels firmly weight-bearing on the ground. For instance, use a 1-2 inch thick board beneath the ball of your foot.

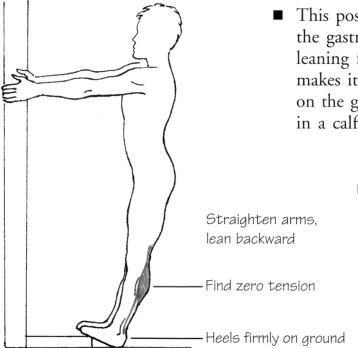

Straighten arms, lean backward

Find zero tension

Heels firmly on ground

- This position enables you to load the gastrocnemius muscle without leaning forward. Leaning forward makes it harder to keep the heels on the ground, which is a *necessity* in a calf-muscle stretch.

- Hold onto the structure in front of you. For example, stand in front of a door so that you can hold onto the door jam.

Find Zero Tension

- Standing straight with the forefoot on the raised surface, you will feel tension behind the knee. This is overstretching, because the tension is in the wrong place.
- *Lean backward*, away from the door jam or whatever you are holding onto, to reduce that muscle tension to zero.

- Leaning backward keeps the heels firmly fixed on the ground, the posture remains straight, and the quadricep muscles can relax without the knees buckling. Do not lock the knees by contracting the quadriceps.
- This is the best position for isolating the gastrocnemius muscles in a position where the muscles can relax and slide longer.

Find the First Awareness

- Once you have reached "zero tension" by leaning backward, slowly pull your body forward with your arms until you feel the first awareness.

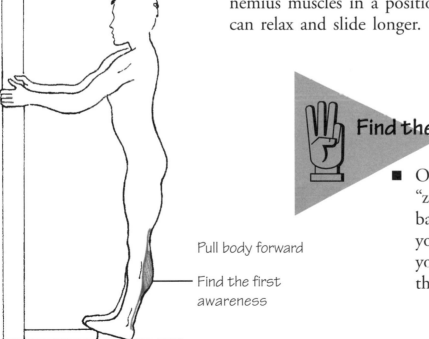

Pull body forward

Find the first awareness

Less is Best

- You have to isolate the first gentle tension, the first awareness, in the middle of the gastrocnemius muscle mass. There should be no sensation of pulling or tension behind the knees.
- The first awareness is subtle! Patience is required until your biofeedback becomes familiar with this gentle tension.

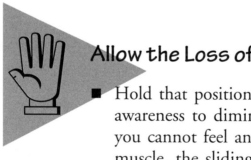

Allow the Loss of Tension

- Hold that position and *allow* that first awareness to diminish and release. When you cannot feel any tension left in the muscle, the sliding elongation (stretch) is completed.

Recommendation:

Repeat the stretch a second time. The only way to gain more length and power is to repeat the process.

A. Advantages of stretching both gastrocnemius muscles at the same time:

There are two reasons for stretching both legs simultaneously. It is the best method of isolating the calf muscles in a proper position where they can relax and elongate, and it also *improves your biofeedback*.

When both legs are loaded at the same time and the first awareness is found, you may feel the tension in only one calf muscle, or one calf muscle slightly more than the other. This is normal. It is the best biofeedback the brain is capable of and the most subtle awareness. The brain is *not registering intensity*, it is *registering the difference in the two muscles*.

When isolating one calf muscle at a time, people routinely load the calf muscle much harder before the biofeedback registers. At the very least the desired effect is delayed, and damage may result.

The secret is knowing *where to feel that gentle tension*, knowing *where not to feel that tension*, and that *less is best*. The more gently you load the muscles, the faster they will relax and slide longer.

IV. GASTROCNEMIUS STRETCH: ONE LEG AT A TIME

Sometimes there is nothing convenient on which to place the ball of the feet for the calf stretch (as described above), loading both calf muscles at the same time. As an alternative this is how to stretch one leg at a time.

■ To isolate the gastrocnemius muscle, it is important to *keep the heel firmly on the ground.* Position the hips over the heel of the leg being stretched, with the hip and leg forming an angle of about 45 degrees, and keep the back straight. This isolates the gastrocnemius muscle with the heel firmly on the ground.

45°

—— Find the first awareness

—— Heels firmly on ground

■ Bend the elbows and the front knee, and lean the whole body toward the wall as a unit. This will increase the tension on the calf muscle, and the hip stays back to ensure that the heel stays firmly on the ground.

■ If the hip angle straightens it becomes harder to keep the heel on the ground.

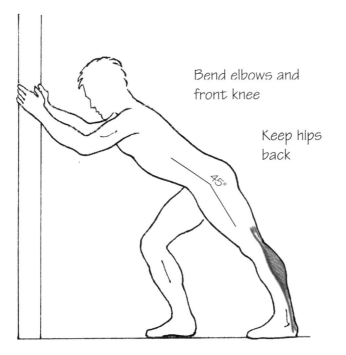

Bend elbows and front knee

Keep hips back

45°

The gastrocnemius muscle cannot relax and slide past its current resting length if it is contracted and expending energy in order to *hold the heel bone in the air.*

V. MISTAKES IN THE GASTROC-NEMIUS MUSCLE STRETCH

A. Overstretching

- When doing a gastrocnemius muscle stretch you should *never feel any pulling or tension behind the knee.* If you do, you are overstretching. The upper muscle-tendon junctions of the gastrocnemius are slightly below the knee and the bulk of the muscle is below the knee.

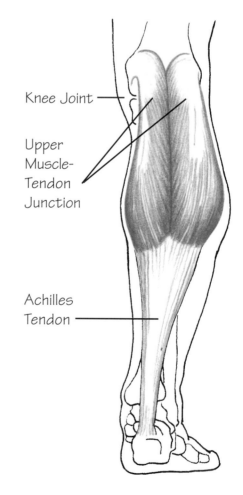

Knee Joint

Upper Muscle-Tendon Junction

Achilles Tendon

- This overloading of the muscle will delay the relaxation/sliding elongation that is the desired effect; and it may cause tearing and scarring at the upper muscle-tendon junction or behind the knee.

■ During the stretch you should never feel any heavy pull in the tendon because it is practically inelastic. NO ONE CAN STRETCH THE ACHILLES TENDON. People who talk about achilles stretches are using old and incorrect terminology. The achilles tendon is a structure composed of very inelastic collagen fiber, and cannot elongate more than 3% without rupture.

■ The farther you lean forward, as demonstrated in this illustration, the more muscles you have to contract to stabilize this position, and the harder it becomes to keep your heel firmly on the ground.

Quadriceps contracted

Heel off the ground

OVERSTRETCHING

The gastrocnemius muscle has demonstrated a myotatic or stretch reflex to stabilize the femur in a standing position to correct an excess shifting of the center of gravity. Some research shows reflex contractions if the angle of the leg over the foot *exceeds forty-five degrees,* even if the heel is on the ground. This is a myotactic response to balance and position, and the gastrocnemius muscle may not relax to the resting length while this position is maintained.

B. Positioning Errors

■ A common mistake is dropping the heels off a step or curb, or leaning forward in a position where the heel comes off the ground. If the heel (calcaneus) is off the ground, the gastrocnemius will remain contracted, expending energy, holding up the bone. This is an isometric contraction by definition. It is *not a stretch*.

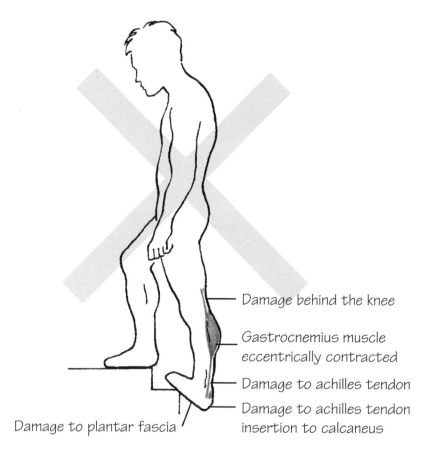

Damage behind the knee

Gastrocnemius muscle eccentrically contracted

Damage to achilles tendon

Damage to achilles tendon insertion to calcaneus

Damage to plantar fascia

- Because the achilles tendon is stronger than the muscle and the bone, it is the muscle fibers and the periosteum of the heel bone that may be torn. This can lead to chronic tearing and damage to the gastrocnemius muscle, as well as inflammation of the heel (calcaneal periostitis) and achilles tendon (tendonitis).

- The large tendinous structure of the foot (*the plantar fascia*) is also put under great stress in this position. Even in healthy people this can cause *plantar fasciitis*, a very common and painful problem. In anyone suffering from plantar fasciitis this improper stretch will only make their problem much worse.

- Some health professionals are prescribing these eccentric drops (the muscles contracted eccentrically to maintain a position) as stretches for treatment of achilles tendonitis and are surprised when their patients' symptoms get worse.

C. Loading Other Structures

■ Other muscles and their tendons are loaded when people place their toes against the wall and lean into that leg until they feel the calf muscles.

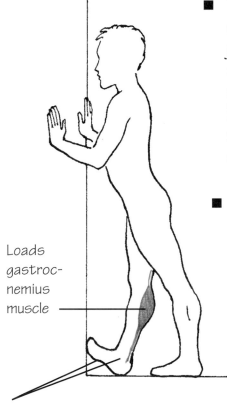

Loads gastroc-nemius muscle

Also loads flexor digitorum longus and flexor hallucis longus muscles

■ The problem with this position is that it creates overloading of the *flexor digitorum longus* and *flexor hallucis longus* muscles (shown in the illustration). These muscles are part of the deep posterior muscle group against the back of the shin bone (tibia). This is a separate muscle compartment located underneath the gastrocnemius and soleus muscles and the achilles tendon.

■ The muscle-tendon junctions of these two very important muscles are underneath the achilles tendon, just behind the ankle bone (medial malleoli). The tendons travel under the medial ankle bone and extend all the way to the bottom (plantar aspect) of the toes.

■ The flexor hallucis longus tendon is attached to the bottom of the big toe (hallux).

■ The flexor digitorum longus tendon divides (bifurcates) into four tendons that attach to the bottom of the four smaller toes.

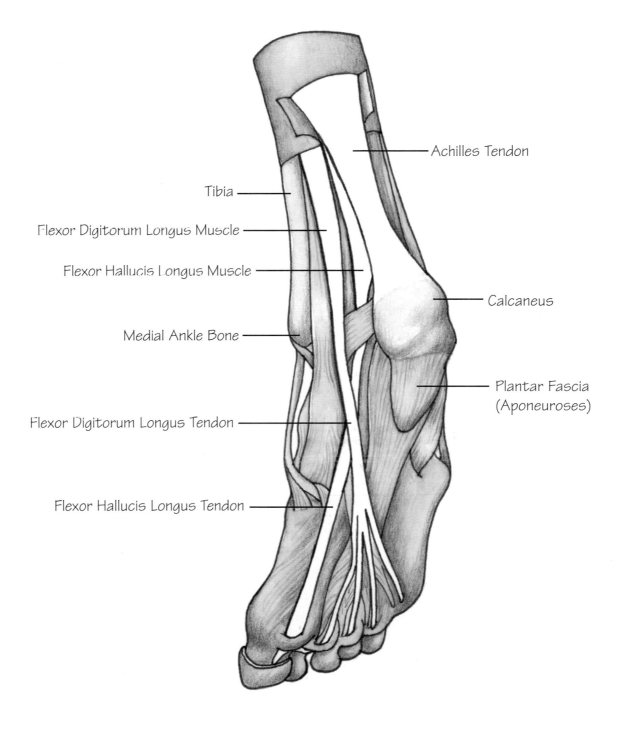

Achilles Tendon

Tibia

Flexor Digitorum Longus Muscle

Flexor Hallucis Longus Muscle

Calcaneus

Medial Ankle Bone

Plantar Fascia
(Aponeuroses)

Flexor Digitorum Longus Tendon

Flexor Hallucis Longus Tendon

- These muscles are the long flexor muscles of the toes that help stabilize the toes against the ground.

  - When the toes of the foot are extended in the position shown in the illustration, these two small muscles are under a great deal of elongation and tension. If the gastrocnemius muscle is then loaded these small muscles will suffer microscopic tearing and damage.

  - This results in damage at the muscle-tendon junction, tightness and inflammation in the two smaller muscles, and *tenosynovitis* of these muscles' tendons.

TENOSYNOVITIS

Discussion:

Anywhere a tendon is under traction as it is pulled around a bone, such as the inside ankle bone (the medial malleolus), the tendon is surrounded by a tendon sheath.

TENOSYNOVITIS

Tenosynovitis is chronic inflammation of the tendon and the tendon sheath caused by *excessive traction of the tendon* around the bone. The excess traction and microscopic tearing results in the formation of fibrous adhesions of the tendon to the tendon (synovial) sheath. When the muscle is contracted and the tendon moves inside the tendon sheath, these adhesions are broken. This causes a very sharp, quick pain in the area.

Many patients come to my clinic with symptoms of pain around the inside of the ankle and up the back of the shin bone underneath the achilles tendon. They complain of pain on the medial aspect of the ankle *underneath* the achilles tendon, with the soreness extending up the posterior medial aspect of the tibial. They assume that this is an achilles tendon problem.

In reality, this is *tenosynovitis of the long flexor muscle tendons and tendon sheaths* often caused by doing the incorrect stretch described above for months. Prolonged tearing and inflammation to the long flexor muscles can lead to a *posterior compartment syndrome.*

VI. SOLEUS MUSCLE

A. Anatomy

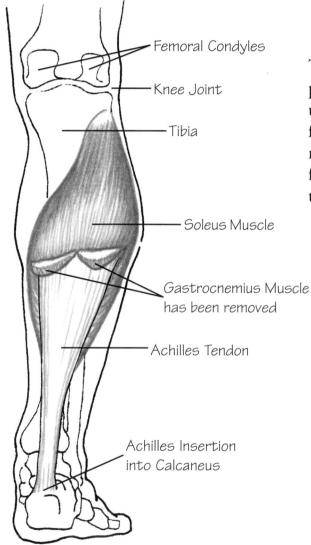

Femoral Condyles

Knee Joint

Tibia

Soleus Muscle

Gastrocnemius Muscle
has been removed

Achilles Tendon

Achilles Insertion
into Calcaneus

The soleus originates from the posterior surface of the head and upper third of the shaft of the fibula, the middle third of the medial border of the tibia, and from a fibrous band between the tibia and fibula.

The soleus terminates into a tendon that joins the tendon of the gastrocnemius in forming the achilles tendon.

VII. Soleus Stretch

The soleus muscle shortens with repetitive usage, as does the gastrocnemius muscle. The two muscles work as a unit, with the soleus functioning with the tibia from which it originates.

- The positioning for the soleus stretch is the same as the gastrocnemius stretch, except that in order to isolate the soleus muscle the knee must be flexed enough (15 to 20 degrees) to unload the gastrocnemius muscle completely.

- The heel should be firmly on the ground.

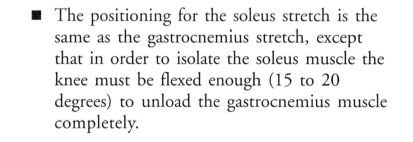

Knee Flexed 15 – 20°

Less Than 45° Angle of Ankle

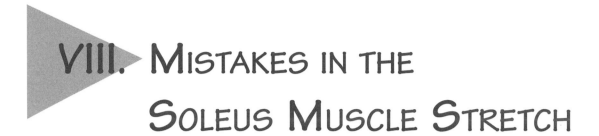

VIII. MISTAKES IN THE SOLEUS MUSCLE STRETCH

A. Positioning Errors

■ The soleus is a very active *muscle of posture*. The farther forward the body weight shifts in front of (anterior) the ankle joint, the more the soleus muscle will *involuntarily* contract (myotactic contracture) to stabilize the tibia and fibula.

Chapter 14

GROIN MUSCLES (ADDUCTORS)

The groin muscles (the adductors) consist of the five muscles on the inside of the thigh (femur).

The five muscles are:

1. the pectineus

2. the adductor longus

3. the adductor brevis

4. the adductor magnus

5. the gracilis

I. GROIN MUSCLES (ADDUCTORS)

A. Anatomy

The groin muscles originate from the bone in the front of the pelvis (pubic rami), and extend down the inside of the leg where they attach to the femur. Only the gracilis muscle tendon crosses the knee joint and attaches to the shin bone (tibia).

B. Biomechanics

These five muscles help stabilize the femur to the pelvis. If these muscles have shortened with repetitive usage and fatigue, they will pull the femur in and the pelvis down in motion, thus increasing knee and back stress.

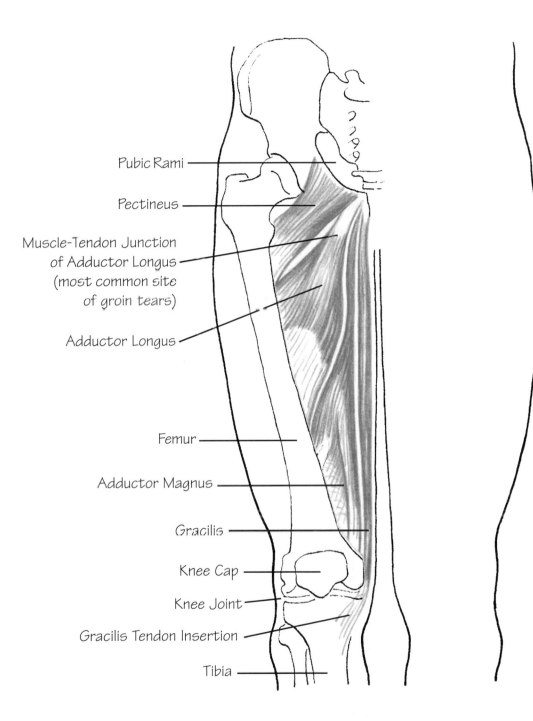

Pubic Rami

Pectineus

Muscle-Tendon Junction
of Adductor Longus
(most common site
of groin tears)

Adductor Longus

Femur

Adductor Magnus

Gracilis

Knee Cap

Knee Joint

Gracilis Tendon Insertion

Tibia

**Groin Muscles (Adductors)
Anterior View – Right Leg**

II. SITTING GROIN STRETCH: (SITTING ADDUCTOR STRETCH)

☝ Isolate the Muscle Group

- To isolate the adductors in the best position to allow them to relax and slide past their current resting length, *the stretch must be done sitting.*

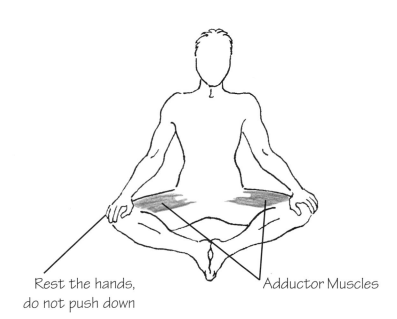

Rest the hands, do not push down

Adductor Muscles

- Rest the back against the wall and place the heels together starting well away from the body. Allow the legs to fall laterally as illustrated. This position isolates the adductor muscles across the hip joint in a position where they are not expending energy to maintain a position.

■ If there is nothing to lean against, use your arms to support the body, and keep the back straight.

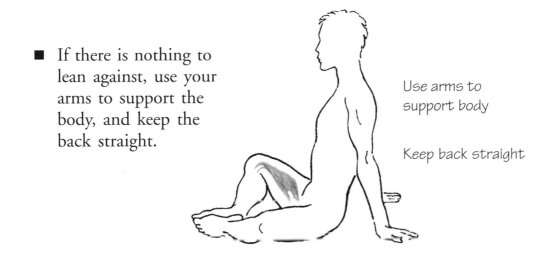

Use arms to support body

Keep back straight

Find Zero Tension

■ Start with the feet and legs far enough from the body so that there is no tension or awareness in the groin muscles.

Find the First Awareness

■ Bring the feet toward the pelvis a little at a time until that first gentle tension is felt in the groin muscles.

Less is Best

- You may feel only one leg initially. Do not go past that point until the tension is gone.
- Symmetry is everything. The goal is to gain more length in the shorter muscle group and more symmetry with the opposite leg.

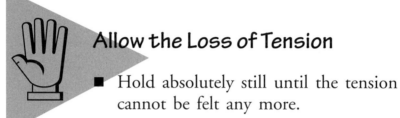

Allow the Loss of Tension

- Hold absolutely still until the tension cannot be felt any more.

III. MISTAKES IN GROIN STRETCHES

A. Overstretching

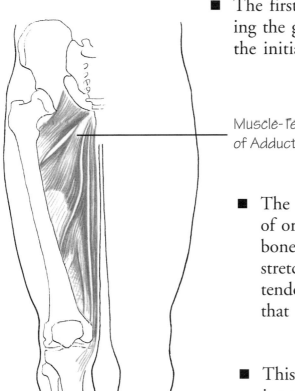

Muscle-Tendon Junction
of Adductor Longus

- The first landmark to learn when stretching the groin muscles is where not to feel the initial tension.

- The adductor longus has a small, thin tendon of origin arising from the front of the pubic bone. Should the initial tension of the groin stretch be felt in the area of this muscle-tendon junction, it is often an overstretch that will result in tearing and scarring.

- This tearing of the upper muscle-tendon junction of the adductor longus muscle is the most common *groin tear* injury in sports.

- If you feel tension in the upper muscle-tendon junction of the adductor longus muscle, reduce the tension by pushing the feet farther away from the body until the tension is felt more in the muscle fibers.

B. Ballistics or Pushing On The Legs

- *Do not bounce the legs or use your hands to push down on the legs.* Every time the leg is bounced, or you push down on the legs, the muscles contract against the loading force.

Do not push down on legs with hands or arms

- This reflex contraction does not allow the muscles to relax back to their current resting length, so they cannot elongate by sliding past their current resting length.

C. Loading Other Structures

(a) Ligaments of the Pelvis

- The large sacrotuberous ligament that originates from the bone of the pelvis that you sit on (the ischial tuberosity) is one of the main stabilizers of the back of the pelvis.

  - Many adults who bend forward from the pelvis with their legs abducted and externally rotated as illustrated in the groin stretch are causing stress and tearing of the ligament structures of the posterior aspect of their pelvis.

(b) Ligaments of the Spine

- Ligaments of the lower lumbar vertebrae of the spine are also loaded when bending forward in the groin stretch.

- Repeated stress over a long period will weaken these structures.

Ligaments of Lumbar Spine
Ligaments of Posterior Pelvis

Loading Stress on Ligament
Structures of the Pelvis and Lower Spine

Many people get up the morning after exercising and "stretching" and wonder why the back of their pelvis or their lowback feels painful. They do not realize this damage and soreness is the result of the inappropriate positioning while stretching the day before.

D. Positioning Errors

- NO ONE can stretch their adductors in the standing position illustrated below.

    - The adductors are involuntarily contracted in this position to stabilize the femur to the pelvis against the pull of gravity.

- This is an involuntary myotactic muscle reflex response to position, balance, and gravity. The adductors cannot be relaxed or the pelvis will fall sideways.

    - If the adductors are voluntarily relaxed, the pelvis will drop and injure the pelvis and/or the femur.

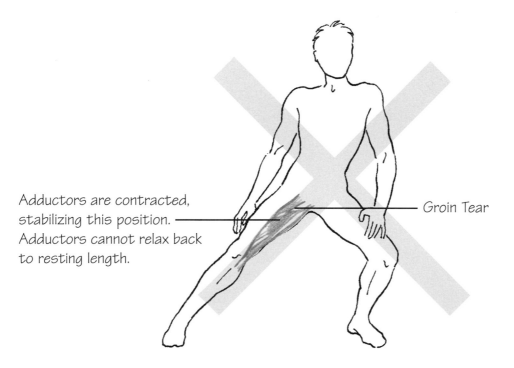

Adductors are contracted, stabilizing this position. Adductors cannot relax back to resting length.

Groin Tear

Example:

Many hockey players try to stretch their groin muscles while *standing* or *moving* on the ice. Their adductor muscles are contracted to help stabilize the thigh to the pelvis. There can be no sliding elongation of the adductor muscles while standing or moving.

When a bounce or ballistic load is added, this often results in the groin tear they are trying to avoid. This damage will result in increased scar tissue and weakening of the muscle-tendon junctions.

Not only do they gain no benefit from their incorrect stretch, they may actually be causing their groin tears. It is astonishing the number of athletes with groin injuries caused by incorrect groin stretches.

NOTES

Chapter 15

QUADRICEPS

The four muscles of the front (anterior) of the thigh are the quadriceps.

The four muscles are:

1. the vastus lateralis
2. the vastus intermedius
3. the vastus medialis
4. the rectus femoris

I. QUADRICEPS

A. Anatomy

The Rectus Femoris, the top muscle (anterior) of the quadriceps group, has a tendon of origin from the front of the pelvis. The other three quadriceps have their tendon of origin from the front of the femur.

All of the quadricep muscles' tendons of insertion combine to form the patella tendon.

B. Biomechanics

The quadriceps' main function is to extend (straighten) the leg and stabilize the knee. This muscle group is an important group in terms of power. Sprinters and cyclists need to develop both *strength* and *power* from their quadricep muscles.

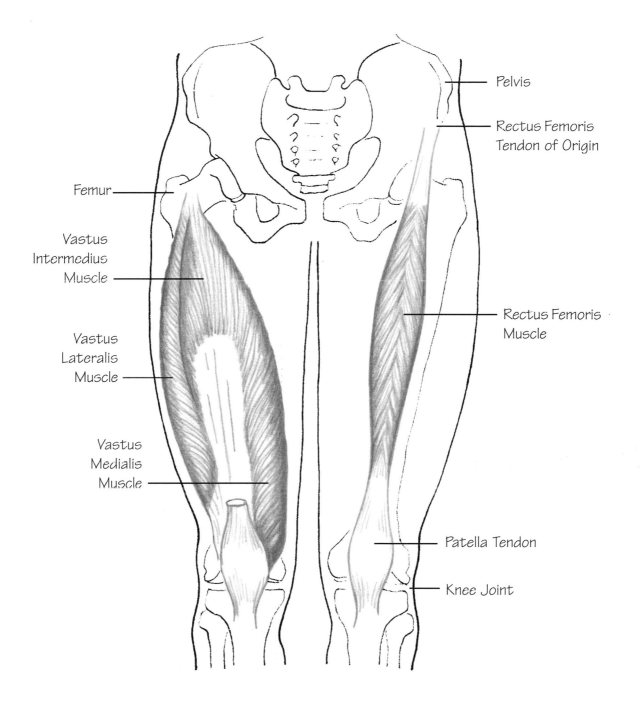

Pelvis

Rectus Femoris
Tendon of Origin

Femur

Vastus
Intermedius
Muscle

Vastus
Lateralis
Muscle

Rectus Femoris
Muscle

Vastus
Medialis
Muscle

Patella Tendon

Knee Joint

**Right Quadriceps with Rectus
Femoris Muscle Removed**

**Left Rectus Femoris
Muscle**

II. QUADRICEPS STRETCH: LYING ON YOUR SIDE

Isolate the Muscle Group

- To isolate the quadriceps, lie on your side as shown in the illustration.
- Flex the knee and hold the *leg* you are stretching just above the ankle; do not hold the foot.

Thigh in Alignment with Body

Find Zero Tension

- Start with the thigh far enough in front of the pelvis that there is no awareness of tension in the quadricep muscles.

Find the First Awareness

- Find the first gentle tension in the middle of the quadriceps by pulling the leg back with your hand.
- Only a few people with good quadriceps length will need to pull the leg behind the pelvis to find the first awareness.

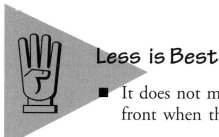

Less is Best

- It does not matter if the leg is still in front when that first tension is found.

Allow the Loss of Tension

- What does matter is that the position is held long enough for the muscles to relax and elongate. The more this muscle group is elongated the farther back the leg will eventually go.
- Repeat with the other leg.

III. STANDING QUADRICEPS STRETCH

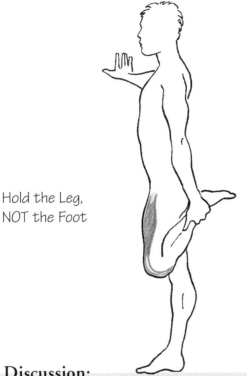

Hold the Leg,
NOT the Foot

- The quadriceps stretch can be done standing in the same manner as described when lying on your side.
- In the standing stretch you have weight-bearing stress on other structures, which decreases the subtlety of your awareness in the quadriceps muscles.
- In addition, most people are not patient enough to allow the time necessary for the muscle relaxation/elongation to occur.

Discussion:

The *rectus femoris* muscle is longer than the other three quadricep muscles, and its tendon of origin is attached to the pelvis. The three other quadriceps originate from tendons attached to the femur. To increase the load on the rectus femoris in both stretches discussed above, a subtle forward tilt of the pelvis is necessary. The forward rotation of the pelvis increases the length from origin to insertion of this particular quadricep muscle. This is done to ensure you are not just loading the three shorter quadriceps muscles in these stretches.

IV. MISTAKES IN QUADRICEPS STRETCHES

A. Positioning Errors

- Don't hold your leg with the opposite hand.

  - When the right leg is held with the left hand the thigh (femur) is externally rotated. This takes the quadriceps out of their proper functional alignment.

- This position also loads at least two of the adductor muscles: the pectineus and the adductor longus. This prevents proper positioning and isolation of the muscle group targeted in the stretch.

B. Loading Other Structures

- When the *foot* is held instead of the *leg* above the ankle while doing a quadriceps stretch, there is a loading force on the long extensor tendons of the toes.

  - These tendons originate from the anterior muscle group of the lower leg, whose tendons of origin are attached to the *lateral ligament structures of the knee.*

■ This is another example of loading muscle groups unrelated to the muscle group you intended to stretch. This can cause minor strain over a long period of time, resulting in chronic, low-level injury to the lateral structures of the knee where this muscle group originates.

■ At the very least, the loading of other structures interferes with the awareness of the quadriceps in the stretch. The isolation of the muscle group and the biofeedback will not be as accurate.

Loading foot increases stress on anterior muscles of the leg

C. Injuries

DO NOT put the knee in a weight-bearing position on the ground for any stretch.

- The knee cap (the patella bone) is part of the patella tendon. The posterior surface of the patella is covered with articular cartilage. When the quadriceps muscles are contracted they extend the knee, using the patella tendon as a pulley system across the knee joint.

  - The articular cartilage on the underside of the patella, gliding over the articular cartilage of the femur, keeps the tendon from fraying and breaking down.

- People that must kneel on the knee cap in a working situation will often develop damage to the articular cartilage of the knee cap and the femur (chondromalacia). This is caused by constantly driving the two articular surfaces against each other with great force. This is an unfortunate occupational hazard.

■ It has become popular to kneel down while holding the foot and loading the quadricep muscles as a stretch. *To do this as a stretch is wrong.*

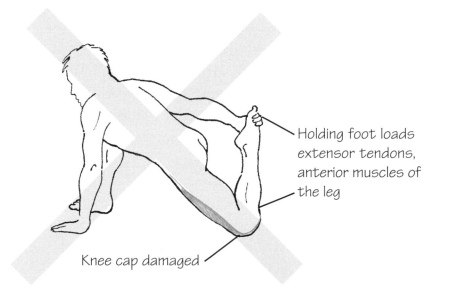

Holding foot loads extensor tendons, anterior muscles of the leg

Knee cap damaged

■ When the quadriceps are loaded with the knee on the ground, traction is applied to the patella tendon that greatly increases the *force of compression* between the knee cap and the femur, causing damage to the articular cartilage of the knee cap and femur.

Chapter 16

HAMSTRINGS

The three muscles of the back
of the thigh are the hamstrings.

The three muscles are:

1. the semitendinosus

2. the semimembranosus

3. the biceps femoris

I. HAMSTRINGS

A. Anatomy

All three hamstring muscles have tendons of origin from the bone you sit on (the ischial tuberosity).

The semitendinosus and the semimembranosus are the medial hamstring muscles, which have tendons of insertion crossing the back of the knee on the inside (medial side).

The biceps femoris muscle is the lateral hamstring whose tendon of insertion crosses the back of the knee on the outside (lateral side).

The lower muscle-tendon junctions of the hamstring muscles are approximately 4-8 inches above your knee, depending on the length of your leg.

There is NO hamstring muscle behind the knee!

B. Biomechanics

The hamstrings extend the thigh (femur) on the pelvis and flex the knee. They are very important muscles in terms of acceleration and jumping. They are also very important muscles of position and posture.

The hamstring muscles can be isolated in a proper stretching position while *sitting or lying on the back.*

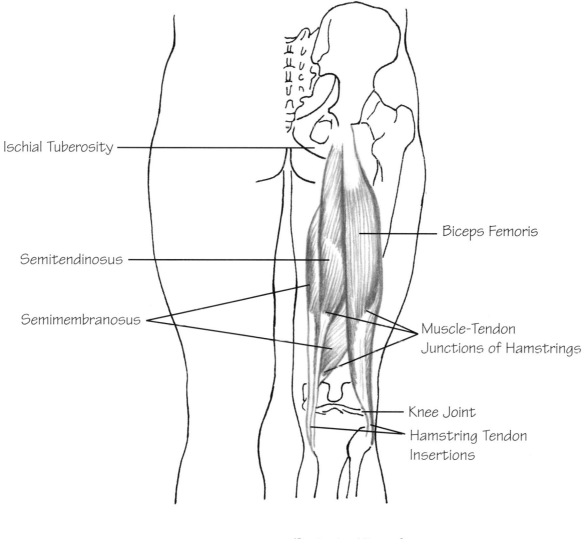

Ischial Tuberosity

Biceps Femoris

Semitendinosus

Semimembranosus

Muscle-Tendon
Junctions of Hamstrings

Knee Joint
Hamstring Tendon
Insertions

**Posterior View of
Right Leg**

II. SITTING HAMSTRING STRETCH

Isolate the Muscle Group

- To isolate the left hamstring muscles in proper sitting position, start with the left leg straight or the knee slightly bent and keep the left leg at a 90° angle to the pelvis.

  - Place the arms on the ground behind the pelvis, and sit with a straight back so that the posterior ligaments of the pelvis and spine are not loaded.

    - Bend (flex) the right knee just enough to allow the right leg to fall sideways as shown.

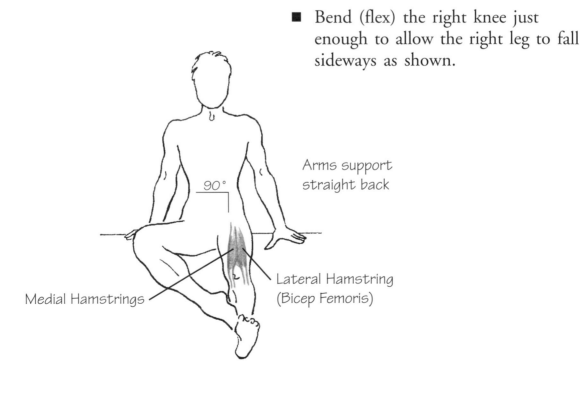

90°

Arms support straight back

Medial Hamstrings

Lateral Hamstring (Bicep Femoris)

Find Zero Tension

■ Move the arms and upper body backward until there is no tension or awareness felt in the hamstrings.

■ Always start where there is no tension or awareness in the hamstrings.

Find the First Awareness

■ Move the arms and upper body forward, maintaining a straight back, and find the first awareness in the hamstrings.

■ Often the first awareness will be felt behind the knee where there are no hamstring muscles. There are only *tendons of the hamstring muscles* behind the knee, and other structures such as the *joint capsule* of the knee.

Keep back straight, stabilize with the palms

No awareness **behind** the knee

■ Reduce the tension in very small increments by moving the arms and upper body backward until the tension is felt only in the hamstrings muscles at least a hand's width above the knee.

■ 137 ■

Less is Best

■ The more gentle the initial muscle load, the faster the muscle will relax back to its resting length.

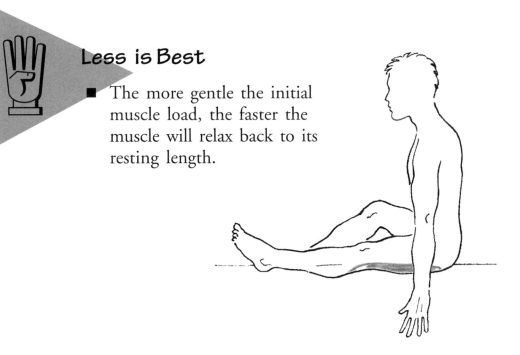

Allow the Loss of Tension

■ The static tension must be held long enough for the relaxation/sliding elongation to happen. Remember, you cannot time stretches.

III. HAMSTRING STRETCHES LYING ON THE BACK

☝ Isolate the Muscle Group

- Lying on the back isolates the hamstring muscles better than sitting, because there is no weight-bearing stress on the pelvis and spine.

- Keep the other knee bent with the foot flat on the floor. This reduces the rotation in the pelvis and negates any load on the hip flexors of the bent leg.

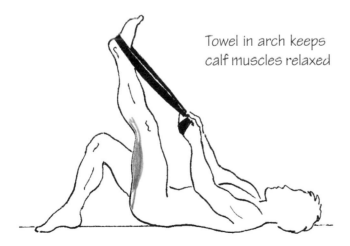

Towel in arch keeps calf muscles relaxed

- The better the isolation, the fewer structures loaded, the better the biofeedback.

Find Zero Tension

- The hands can be used to gently support the leg, but it is better isolation to use a towel or a belt to hold the leg as illustrated.

    - MAKE SURE that the towel is in the arch of the foot like a stirrup so the forefoot is not loaded, causing the calf muscle to tighten.

Find the First Awareness

- Find the first awareness in the hamstring muscles by pulling the leg toward your head. If the first awareness is close to or behind the knee, gradually reduce the tension until the tension moves into the muscle fibers of the hamstrings.

Less is Best

- The more gentle the initial muscle load, the faster the muscle will relax back to its resting length.

Allow the Loss of Tension

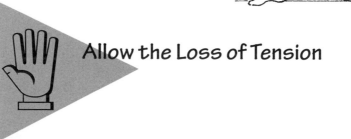

IV. THE WALL STRETCH

People with very tight hamstring muscles can isolate their hamstrings by lying flat on the ground and placing the heels of the feet on a wall. In this position the wall holds the legs, so there is less strain on the arms. The hamstrings can be isolated in a position where they can relax and slide past their resting length in a comfortable position.

■ The tension in the hamstrings is adjusted by two methods in this position.

   ■ Larger adjustments of the tension on the hamstring muscles are made by sliding the hips closer to the wall to increase the tension, or away from the wall to decrease the tension.

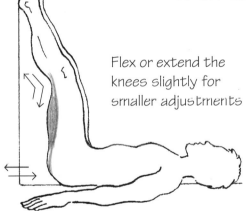

Flex or extend the knees slightly for smaller adjustments

   ■ Smaller, more subtle adjustments can be made by straightening (extending) the knee for more tension, or bending (flexing) the knee for less tension.

   ■ Because all three hamstring tendons cross the back of the knee, *all hamstring stretches* should take advantage of the knee movement to adjust the muscle tension.

Move hips closer or farther from the wall for larger adjustments

■ The rules of where and where not to feel the tension do not change, regardless of which proper position you choose as a stretch. Remember, do not feel any tension behind the knee, because there is no hamstring muscle behind the knee.

V. ISOLATING THE MEDIAL OR LATERAL HAMSTRINGS

The medial or lateral hamstring muscles can be isolated in any of the proper stretches discussed here. This not only allows you to concentrate on a specific hamstring muscle when it has a problem, it gives you the ability to test your hamstrings and identify an imbalance before a serious problem occurs.

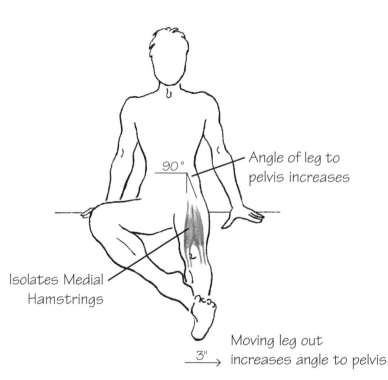

90°

Angle of leg to pelvis increases

Isolates Medial Hamstrings

3"

Moving leg out increases angle to pelvis

Isolate Medial Hamstrings

■ To isolate the medial hamstrings, move the leg out about three inches, widening the angle of the leg to the pelvis. This increases the length of origin to insertion of the medial hamstring muscles (semimembranosus and semitendinosus muscles). Most people can do this with no change in muscle tension, or the tension moves slightly to the inside (medially) of the hamstrings.

■ To isolate the lateral hamstring, move the leg in about three inches, decreasing the angle of the leg to the pelvis. This increases the length of origin to insertion of the lateral hamstring muscle (biceps femoris). Most people will feel more tension and feel the tension move toward the back of the knee because the lateral hamstring is often tighter than the medial hamstrings.

■ Continue isolating the lateral hamstring and reduce the tension in the muscle until the tension is felt only in the muscle fibers well above the knee.

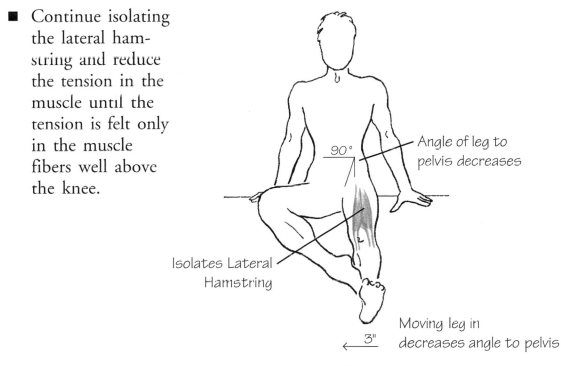

Isolate Lateral Hamstrings

The reason most people feel a greater tension when they move the leg medially to isolate the lateral hamstring (biceps femoris muscle) is because the traditional stretch often taught is incorrect, and places more tension on the medial hamstrings.

VI. MISTAKES IN HAMSTRING STRETCHES

A. Positioning Errors

- As described previously, increasing the angle of the leg to the pelvis during a hamstring stretch isolates the medial hamstrings. Spreading the legs increases the length of origin to insertion and places more tension on the medial hamstrings (semitendinosus and semimembranosus muscles). The length of origin to insertion and the tension on the lateral hamstring is decreased.

- Just as spreading the legs increases the angle of the leg to the pelvis, pulling the other leg up toward the pelvis increases the angle of the pelvis to the leg that is being stretched. Both of these are training errors and should be avoided.

- In the position illustrated, the medial hamstrings of the right leg are placed under more tension. This is the reason so many athletes have tight lateral hamstrings.

- In the sitting stretch, start with the opposite leg flexed and out of the way, but keep the pelvis at 90° or less to the leg that you are stretching.

Pulling the left leg this far toward the pelvis rotates the pelvis away from the right leg

B. Loading Other Structures

1. The sitting stretch can damage the posterior ligaments of the lumbar spine and the pelvis if you lean too far forward in this position. Leaning forward increases the loading stress on these ligaments, resulting in insidious tearing and scarring of these structures.

Even if no damage is caused to these structures, the loading of the ligament structures interferes with the biofeedback from the hamstrings.

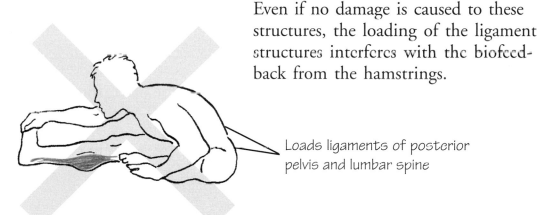

Loads ligaments of posterior pelvis and lumbar spine

2. Never do a hamstring stretch with the opposite knee weight-bearing on the ground in the position illustrated below. This causes tearing, scarring, and weakening of the medial ligaments of the knee joint.

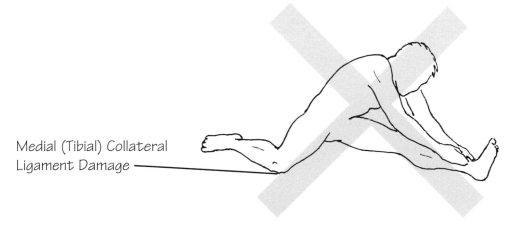

Medial (Tibial) Collateral Ligament Damage

3. Never grab the toes in a hamstring stretch. The gastrocnemius muscle tendons of origin begin above the knee, and the hamstring tendons of insertion all attach to the tibia below the knee. When the calf muscles are placed under loading force simultaneously with the hamstring muscles, the structure often mistakenly loaded and damaged is the posterior joint capsule of the knee.

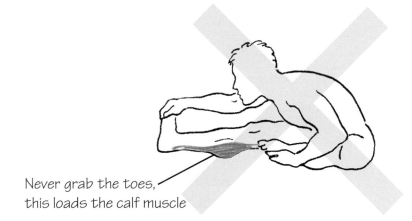

Never grab the toes,
this loads the calf muscle

In this position, ask anyone where they feel "the stretch"; and they always point to BEHIND THE KNEE.

Never load two muscle groups across the same joint at the same time in a *primary stretch*.

C. Incorrect Positioning Due to Involuntary Muscle Contraction

(a) All Standing Hamstring Stretches

There are many examples of improper hamstring stretches. A close look at what the hamstrings do involuntarily in reflex response to standing and bending forward will explain why all standing hamstring stretches are not only wrong, but damage other structures.

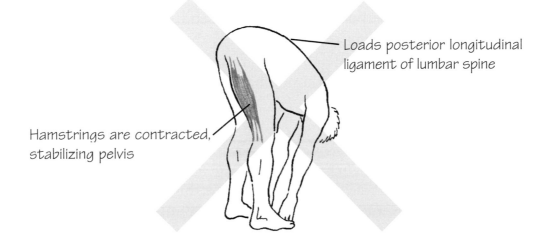

Loads posterior longitudinal ligament of lumbar spine

Hamstrings are contracted, stabilizing pelvis

FACT: When a person is standing and bends forward from the pelvis, the hamstring muscles involuntarily contract (myotactic reflex) to stabilize the pelvis against gravity. The hamstrings will remain contracted, stabilizing the pelvis, as long as the person remains bent forward from the hips.

The hamstrings cannot be stretched in any standing position, because they are contracted and expending energy to stabilize the pelvis against the pull of gravity.

When the hamstrings have contracted to their longest eccentric length (eccentric capacity), the pelvis stops rotating forward.

If the person continues to bend forward, they do so by rounding the lower back as they reach for the ground. This transfers loading force into the posterior longitudinal ligament of the lumbar spine.

This will cause tearing, weakening, and lengthening of the posterior longitudinal ligament that stabilizes the spinal vertebrae and spinal disk. As this ligament weakens over a period of years, the instability can lead to hypermobility of the spine and secondary damage, such as a *herniated disk*.

The damage to these ligament structures is insidious, cumulative, and permanent. The resulting spine and sciatic nerve problems may not become symptomatic until years after the initial damage began.

(b) Ballet Bar Stretches

The ballet bar stretch, where one leg is resting on a chair or a bar or a bench, is also a very damaging position. Again the damage is slow, insidious, and permanent.

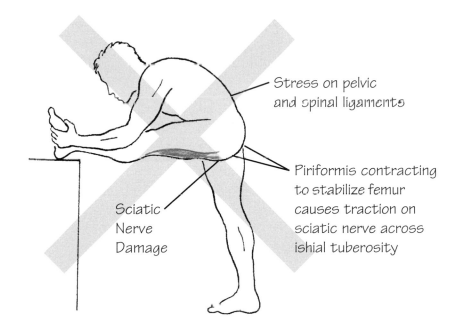

Stress on pelvic and spinal ligaments

Piriformis contracting to stabilize femur causes traction on sciatic nerve across ishial tuberosity

Sciatic Nerve Damage

Both legs are weight-bearing in this position and the person is bending forward from the pelvis. There is good evidence that this also causes a reflex contraction of the hamstring group of both legs to stabilize the pelvis.

In addition, because the femur has rotated on the pelvis and is weight-bearing, the external hip rotators, including the piriformis muscle, are contracted to stabilize the femur. The piriformis muscle anchors the sciatic nerve roots in the posterior hip, especially S3 and S2, and the sciatic nerve plexus is pulled across the bone you sit on (the ischial tuberosity).

This is called the piriformis syndrome in some studies of sciatic nerve damage.

This repetitive traction of the sciatic nerve is one of the causes of sciatic nerve damage (sciatica or neuropraxic stretching injury). Many young athletes initiate this damage at age eight or nine, but do not become symptomatic until they are much older.

Chapter 17

POSTERIOR HIP MUSCLES

(GLUTEUS MAXIMUS & THE EXTERNAL HIP ROTATORS)

The posterior muscles of the hip are the gluteal muscles and the external hip rotator muscles of the femur.

The gluteal muscles are the gluteus maximus, gluteus medius, and the gluteus minimus.

The external hip rotator muscles are the piriformis, the obturator internus, the obturator externus, the gemellus superior, the gemellus inferior, and the quadratus femoris.

I. GLUTEUS MAXIMUS MUSCLE

A. Anatomy

The gluteus maximus is the largest and most prominent muscle of the back of the hip. It has its tendon of origin attached to many structures of the posterior pelvis. Most of its tendon of insertion is attached to the iliotibial tract (I.T. Band).

B. Biomechanics

The gluteus maximus is the major muscle of the iliotibial band. The iliotibial band stabilizes the knee from the lateral side, and is the largest tendinous structure of the body.

Muscles of the Iliotibial Band

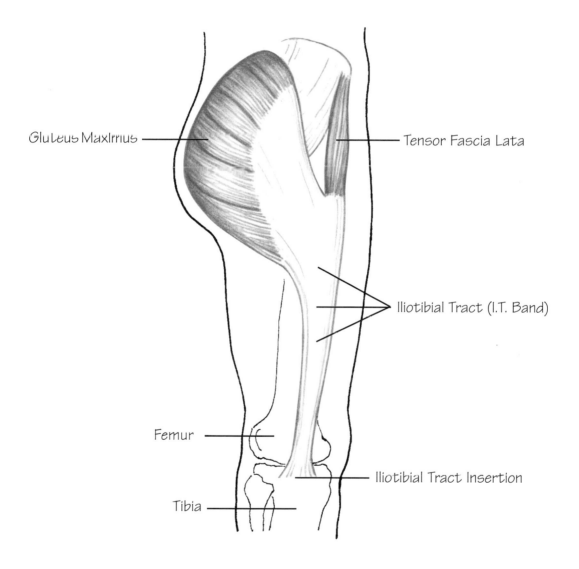

Gluteus Maximus

Tensor Fascia Lata

Iliotibial Tract (I.T. Band)

Femur

Iliotibial Tract Insertion

Tibia

Lateral View of Right Leg

II. EXTERNAL HIP ROTATOR MUSCLES

A. Anatomy

The six smaller muscles beneath the gluteal muscles are the external hip rotators. These small muscles originate from the tail-bone area (the sacrum), cross the back of the pelvis and the sacroiliac joint, and have tendons of insertion attaching to the posterior aspect of the hip bone (the greater trochanter of the femur).

B. Biomechanics

These are the muscles that stabilize the top of the femur in motion, and which turn the femur externally on the pelvis. Some of these smaller muscles cannot be seen from the posterior view in the illustration. They are beneath the more posterior muscles.

The most important of the external hip rotators is the piriformis muscle. The origin of the piriformis muscle is on the anterior surface of the sacrum in the intrapelvic cavity.

External Hip Rotators

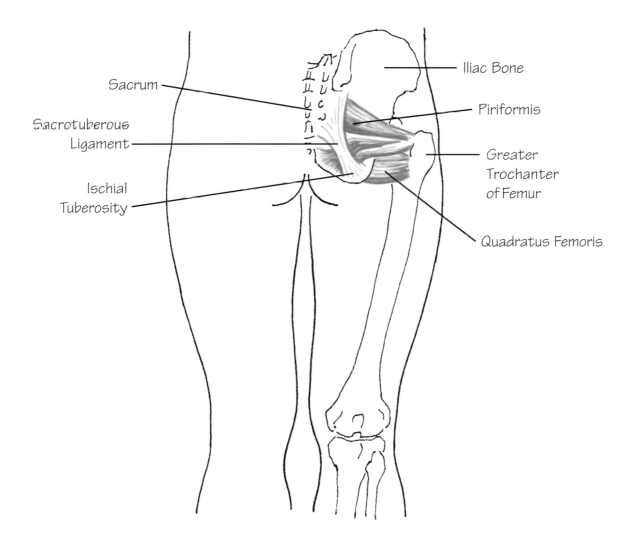

Sacrum

Sacrotuberous
Ligament

Ischial
Tuberosity

Iliac Bone

Piriformis

Greater
Trochanter
of Femur

Quadratus Femoris

Posterior View of Right Leg

III. RELATIONSHIP OF THE POSTERIOR HIP MUSCLES AND THE SCIATIC NERVE ROOTS

Two of the five sciatic nerve roots which form the sciatic nerve plexus, S2 and S3, often pass through the origin of the piriformis muscle (Grant's Atlas, 1972).

The sciatic nerve relationship with the piriformis muscle varies from person to person. In some cases, one or both parts of the sciatic nerve can perforate the piriformis, while in others it passes above or below the muscle; it may even split and pass around the muscle (Janse, 1976; Kendall, Kendall, & Boynton, 1952; Lewin, 1944).

The sciatic nerve roots S2 and S3 have branches separating after passing through the piriformis muscle to become the pudendal nerves to the pelvic cavity. The piriformis muscle cannot be in spasm or excessive tightness for a prolonged period without causing traction on the sciatic and pudendal nerves, resulting in secondary nerve dysfunction.

Long-term symptoms of sciatic nerve damage (sciatica) include everything from numbness and weakness to pain and muscle spasms, especially in the muscles of the posterior hip and down the back of the leg, depending on what portion of the nerve roots are damaged.

Origin of Piriformis Muscle, Sciatic Nerve Roots

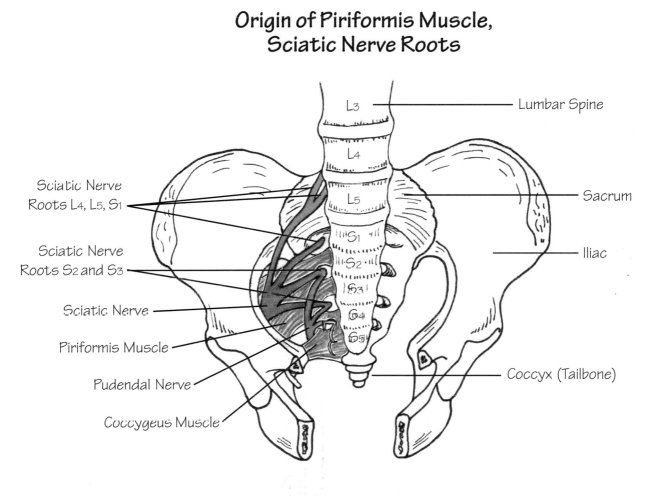

Anterior View of Sacrum

Damage to the pudendal nerve can cause *loss of bladder control, bowel functions, even sexual dysfunction.* It is not uncommon to see patients that have had increasing sciatic nerve problems and hip pain also complaining of periodic episodes of *incontinence.*

NERVE DAMAGE

Interference with reproductive function has been indicated. This is attributed to damage to the pudendal nerves and blood vessels (Retzlaff et al., 1974).

Because of the interrelationship of the posterior hip muscles, especially the piriformis muscle and the sciatic nerve roots, this stretch is of great importance to anyone that has lowback problems, sacroiliac joint and pelvic pain, and of course sciatic nerve problems.

It is sadly overlooked or done incorrectly in many treatment therapies.

IV. GLUTEUS MAXIMUS AND EXTERNAL HIP ROTATOR STRETCH

Isolate the Muscle Group

- The best position to isolate the gluteus maximus and the external hip rotators of the right hip is lying flat on the back. Keep the left foot flat on the ground with the knee bent (flexed). Cross the right leg as illustrated.

- This position isolates the large muscle of the iliotibial band (gluteus maximus) and the six smaller muscles crossing the back of the pelvis (external hip rotators) to attach to the back of the hip bone (greater trochanter of the femur).

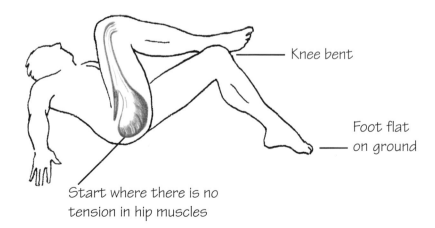

Knee bent

Foot flat
on ground

Start where there is no
tension in hip muscles

Find Zero Tension

- If you feel tension in the posterior hip muscles of the right leg, gradually move the left foot farther away from your body until there is no tension.

Find the First Awareness

- Gradually bring the left foot toward the buttocks until you feel the first awareness of tension in the posterior muscles of the right hip.

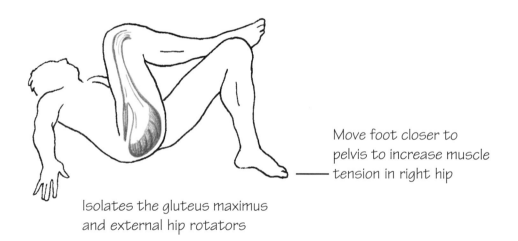

Move foot closer to pelvis to increase muscle tension in right hip

Isolates the gluteus maximus and external hip rotators

- If the first awareness has not been found when the left foot is as close to the body as possible, lift the left leg off the ground until you find the first awareness of tension in the right hip muscles.

■ Use your hands to lift the leg, grasping the thigh just beneath the knee. If you find that you must lift your upper back and head off the ground to reach the thigh, you can use a towel behind the thigh. Pull on the towel with your hands to lift the leg.

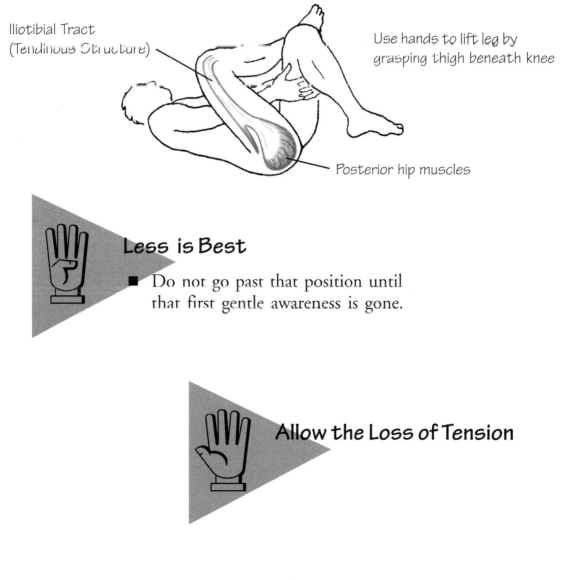

Iliotibial Tract
(Tendinous Structure)

Use hands to lift leg by grasping thigh beneath knee

Posterior hip muscles

Less is Best

■ Do not go past that position until that first gentle awareness is gone.

Allow the Loss of Tension

V. MISTAKES IN POSTERIOR HIP MUSCLE STRETCHES

A. Overstretching

Referring to the illustrations of these structures it is evident that you should not feel anything down the outside of the leg of the posterior hip muscles you want to stretch. There is no muscle in the iliotibial band. It is an inelastic collagen structure, really a large tendon. If you feel a tension down the outside of the leg, you are overstretching and may cause microscopic tearing.

Posterior hip muscles are contracted to stabilize position

B. Positioning Errors

Many people are taught to lean into the wall with their hips rotated sideways as illustrated. *This is not a stretch*. When leaning sideways in a standing position, both muscles of the iliotibial band contract to stabilize the knee from the lateral side. The external hip rotators contract to stabilize the posterior aspect of the femur in this position.

Once again, this a position where these muscles are contracted in response to gravity and balance. They cannot relax because they are stabilizing this weight-bearing position. This position can cause tearing of the iliotibial band insertion in the lateral aspect of the tibia and also pain in the hip from the friction of the hip bone (greater trochanter) underneath the iliotibial band.

C. Loading Other Structures

Sitting and pulling the hips sideways is often a problem, especially if the ischial tuberosity (the bone you are sitting on) is lifted off the ground. This will cause traction of the sciatic nerve underneath the ischial tuberosity.

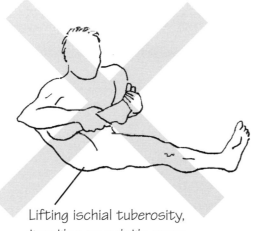

Lifting ischial tuberosity, traction on sciatic nerve

Sitting and twisting the pelvis and spine in one
direction while pulling the left leg across the
pelvis causes the external hip rotators to contract.
This places traction on the proximal nerve roots
of the sciatic nerve.

The sciatic nerve trunk passes beneath the bone you
are sitting on (the ischial tuberosity). With the
proximal nerve roots under traction, especially S2
and S3 which often pass through the piriformis
muscle, and the nerve trunk being pulled under the
ischial tuberosity, this position can cause sciatic
nerve damage.

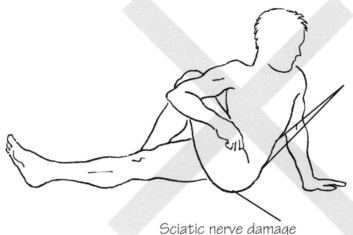

Weight-bearing load
and rotational stress
on ligament structures
of pelvis and spine

Sciatic nerve damage

In the sitting position there is also unnecessary
weight-bearing stress and rotation on the *ligaments*
of the pelvis and spine. This is *unnecessary in order to
stretch this muscle group*, and may cause damage.

Chapter 18

HIP FLEXORS
(Psoas and the Iliacus Muscles)

The hip flexors are comprised of two muscles, the psoas and the iliacus. Together these two muscles form one of the strongest muscle groups in the body.

I. PSOAS AND ILIACUS MUSCLES

A. Anatomy

(a) Psoas Muscle

The psoas is a very long muscle whose tendons of origin are anchored to the anterior/lateral portion of the entire lower spine. These tendons originate on the anterior surface of the transverse processes, the lateral borders of the vertebral bodies, and the corresponding *intervertebral disks* of the spine from *T12* through *L5*.

The psoas separates from the spine at the 5th lumbar vertebrae and transverses through the pelvic girdle, passes under the inguinal ligament in front of the capsule of the hip joint, and its tendon of insertion attaches to the inside of the thigh bone (the lesser trochanter of the femur).

Psoas and Iliacus Muscles

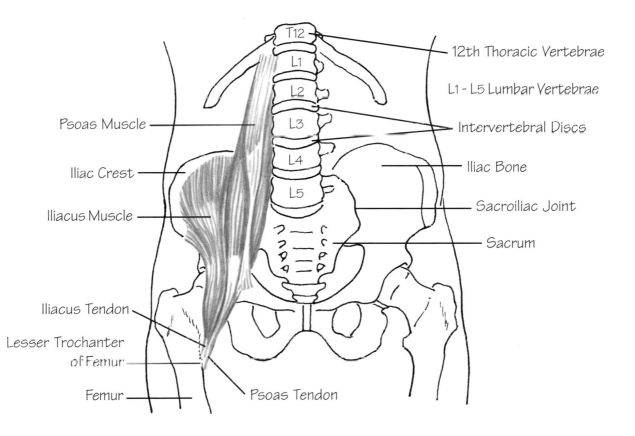

12th Thoracic Vertebrae

L1 - L5 Lumbar Vertebrae

Intervertebral Discs

Iliac Bone

Sacroiliac Joint

Sacrum

Psoas Muscle

Iliac Crest

Iliacus Muscle

Iliacus Tendon

Lesser Trochanter of Femur

Femur

Psoas Tendon

Anterior View of the Lower Spine, Pelvic Girdle and Femurs

(b) Iliacus Muscle

The iliacus muscle originates from tendons that are anchored to the inside of the pelvis, with tendinous slips coming off many of the structures that hold the posterior/lateral aspect of the pelvis together. These tendons originate from the upper two-thirds of the iliac fossa, the internal border of the iliac crest, the anterior sacroiliac, lumbrosacral and iliolumbar ligaments, and the ala of the sacrum.

The iliacus also passes beneath the inguinal ligament, where most of its tendon of insertion converges into the lateral/dorsal side of the tendon of the psoas, with the tendon of insertion ultimately inserting into the inside of the lesser trochanter of the femur.

B. Biomechanics

The iliopsoas complex (hip flexors) are the muscle group that is the prime mover when you lift the thigh to the trunk, and when you bend the trunk to the thigh, *as in sitting up from a prone position*. This is why full sit-ups, especially fixed-leg sit-ups, are not a good abdominal exercise. The hip flexors are the prime movers in this exercise, and have the mechanical advantage necessary to lift the trunk toward the legs.

The farther in front of the axis of the hip joint the upper body is, and the more extended the femur is behind the axis of the hip joint, *the more postural contraction in the hip flexors.*

The hip flexors play an important role in postural balance, and are active in the relaxed standing position (Basmajian, 1978; Greenlaw, 1973; Shy Yan Ng, 1978).

Runner's "Stretch"

This is precisely why the "runner's stretch" illustrated here is another example of a dynamic contraction, *not a stretch*. In this position the hip flexors are contracted, doing work, and expending energy in order to stabilize the trunk on the lower extremity.

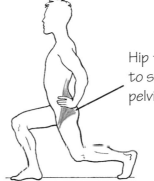

Hip flexors contracted to stabilize femur to pelvis and spine

A Good Mobilization Exercise

Taking the muscles of a muscle group to their longest length of contraction is a *good mobilization exercise*, and will keep the sarcomeres at the ends of the muscles functioning. As discussed in the segment on dynamic "stretches," one can even increase the amount of sarcomeres at the ends of the muscle in this fashion.

II. HIP FLEXOR STRETCH

A. Stretching Alone

Isolate the Muscle Group

■ To isolate the hip flexors (the iliopsoas complex), in a position where they can relax and slide past their resting length, lay flat on your back (supine) on a table.

■ In this position the femur is allowed to abduct and drop, placing a mild tension on the iliopsoas complex.

■ It is vital that the lumbar spine remain flat on the table. If the lowback arches off the table, the pull of the psoas muscle on the vertebrae and the intervertebral disk is increased. This may cause injury to the intervertebral disk.

■ Having the opposite leg held firmly to the chest while doing this stretch helps keep the lowback flat on the table.

■ In this position it is hard to isolate the hip flexors because the hanging leg loads other muscle groups. The sartorius and gracilis muscles are loaded, and to a lesser degree the quadriceps muscles.

■ Although this is the only position I am aware of to isolate the hip flexors, I remain unconvinced that anyone can truly isolate the hip flexors enough to benefit from this stretch when doing it alone.

B. Stretching with a Partner

- With a partner assisting you, the lower leg is held with the knee slightly flexed. With the lower leg supported, the other muscle groups can be minimized or eliminated, and you gain better isolation of the hip flexors.

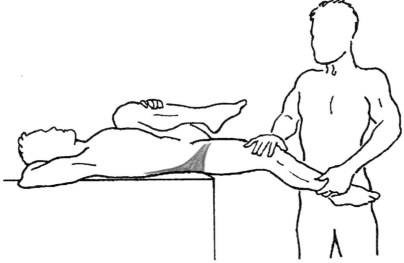

Find Zero Tension

- The partner supports the lower leg by holding the leg at the ankle, keeping the knee slightly bent. This stops the loading of the sartorius, gracilis, and rectus femoris muscles. As always, start where there is no awareness of tension in the hip flexors.

Find the First Awareness

■ The partner can then place a light load on the hip flexors by pushing down and out gently on the thigh with the other hand.

Less is Best

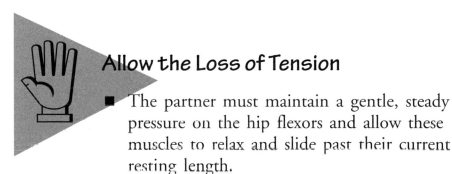

Allow the Loss of Tension

■ The partner must maintain a gentle, steady pressure on the hip flexors and allow these muscles to relax and slide past their current resting length.

CAUTION-CAUTION-CAUTION

This is a difficult stretch, and can cause a great deal of harm if done incorrectly. We advise people not to attempt it without professional help.

NOTES

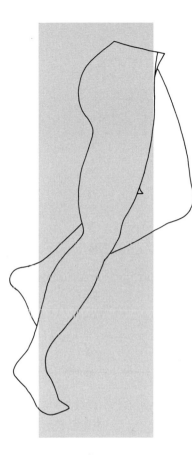

SECTION 4

Easy Reference to Correct Stretches

This section is a quick-reference guide for the reader. Included are the five most practical primary stretches of the weight-bearing muscle groups of the lower extremity for everyone.

As stated previously, a primary stretch is the best stretching position to isolate one muscle group across one joint in a position where that muscle group can relax and slide past their current resting length. This position does not place a significant load on other structures such as the ligaments of joints or the sciatic nerve.

Several of these major muscle groups have more than one proper stretching position. The hamstrings for example, can be stretched sitting or lying on your back. For these muscle groups the stretching position that is the most useful for all ages and for people with extremely tight muscle groups has been chosen.

Anyone that has questions about other positions, the anatomy of the muscle group, the landmarks of good soreness/bad soreness, etc., should refer back to the extensive information in Section 3.

The soleus muscle and the hip flexors (the psoas and the iliacus muscles) are not included in this section. I have reservations about the importance and the positioning of the soleus stretch. I certainly believe that the hip flexor stretch needs to be done carefully, and only after reviewing all the information in Section 3.

Also, it is important for everyone to remember to warm up before stretching.

I. GASTROCNEMIUS STRETCH: BOTH LEGS AT THE SAME TIME

Isolate the Muscle Group

■ The best position to isolate the gastrocnemius muscles is standing with the entire ball of both feet resting on a raised surface and the heels firmly weight-bearing on the ground.

Find Zero Tension

■ Lean backward, away from the door frame or whatever you are holding onto, to reduce the gastrocnemius muscle tension to zero.

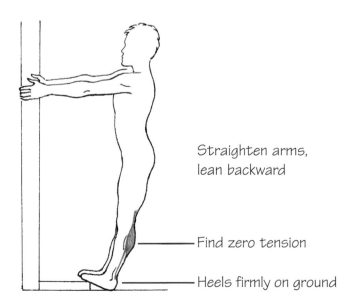

Straighten arms, lean backward

Find zero tension

Heels firmly on ground

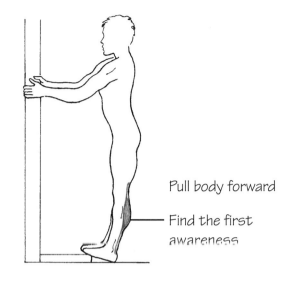

Find the First Awareness

- Once you have reached "zero tension" by leaning backward, slowly pull your body forward with your arms until you feel the first gentle tension in the middle of the gastrocnemius muscles.

Pull body forward

Find the first awareness

Less is Best

- There should be no sensation of pulling or tension behind the knee.
- You will usually feel one gastrocnemius muscle more than the other. The difference you feel is the best biofeedback of these muscles you can have.
- Don't go past that point until the tension is gone.

Allow the Loss of Tension

- Hold that position and allow that first tension to diminish and release.
- Repeat the sequence by pulling forward and finding the second gentle tension in the calf muscles.

II. SITTING GROIN STRETCH: (SITTING ADDUCTOR STRETCH)

☝ Isolate the Muscle Group

- To isolate the adductors the stretch should be done sitting.
- Rest the back against a wall and place the heels together, allowing the legs to fall laterally as illustrated.
- If there is nothing to lean your back against, use your arms to support the body, and keep the back straight.

Use arms to support body

Keep back straight

Rest the hands, do not push down

Adductor Muscles

✌ Find Zero Tension

- Start with the feet far enough from the body that there is no awareness of tension in the groin muscles.

Find the First Awareness

- Bring the feet toward the pelvis a little at a time until that first gentle tension is felt in the groin muscles.

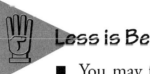

Less is Best

- You may feel tension only in one leg initially. That leg has the shorter muscle group. Do not change position until the tension is gone.
- The goal is more length in the shorter muscle group and more symmetry with the opposite leg.

Allow the Loss of Tension

- Hold completely still until the tension in the groin muscle can no longer be felt.
- Repeat the stretch a second time.

III. QUADRICEPS STRETCH: LYING ON YOUR SIDE

 ## Isolate the Muscle Group

- The best position to isolate the quadriceps is lying on your side, as illustrated.
- Flex the knee and hold the leg you are stretching just above the ankle; do not hold the foot.

Thigh in Alignment with Body

 ## Find Zero Tension

- Start with the thigh far enough in front of the pelvis that there is no awareness of tension in the quadricep muscles.

Find the First Awareness

- Find the first gentle tension in the middle of the quadriceps by pulling the leg back with your hand.
- Only a few people with excellent quadriceps length will need to pull the leg behind the pelvis to find the first awareness.

Less is Best

- The position of the leg when you find the first tension does not matter.

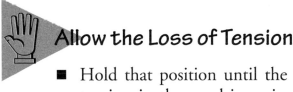

Allow the Loss of Tension

- Hold that position until the tension in the quadriceps is gone.
- Repeat this sequence with the other leg.

IV. SITTING HAMSTRING STRETCH

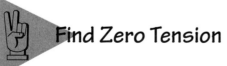 **Isolate the Muscle Group**

- To isolate the left hamstring muscles, sit in the position illustrated.
- The left leg should be at a 90-degree angle to the pelvis.
- Use the arms to support the upper body with the back straight.

90°

Lateral Hamstring
(Bicep Femoris)

Medial Hamstrings

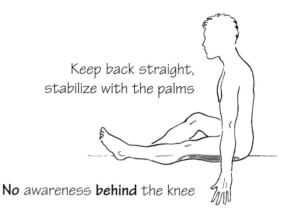

Keep back straight,
stabilize with the palms

No awareness **behind** the knee

Find Zero Tension

- Move the arms and upper body backward until there is no awareness of tension in the hamstrings.

Find the First Awareness

- Move the arms and upper body forward to find the first awareness of tension in the hamstrings.
- Keep the head up and the back straight.

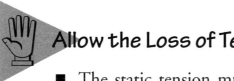

Less is Best

- There should be no tension behind the knee. The first awareness should be felt in the muscles well above the knee joint.

Allow the Loss of Tension

- The static tension must be held long enough for the relaxation/sliding elongation to happen.
- Repeat this sequence with the other leg.

V. GLUTEUS MAXIMUS AND EXTERNAL HIP ROTATOR STRETCH

Isolate the Muscle Group

- The best position to isolate the gluteus maximus and the external hip rotators of the right hip is lying flat on your back as illustrated

Start where there is no tension in hip muscles

Find Zero Tension

- If you feel tension in the posterior muscles of the right hip, gradually move the left foot farther from your body until there is no tension.

Isolates the gluteus maximus and external hip rotators

Find the First Awareness

- Gradually bring the left foot toward the pelvis until you feel the first awareness of tension in the posterior muscles of the right hip.

Less is Best

■ Do not go past that position until that first gentle tension is gone.

■ If the first tension has not been found in the posterior muscles of the right hip when the left foot is as close to the body as possible, you must lift the left leg off the ground until you find the first awareness in the right hip muscles.

Use hands to lift leg by grasping thigh beneath knee

■ Use your hands to lift the leg, grasping the thigh just beneath the knee as illustrated.

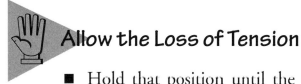

Allow the Loss of Tension

■ Hold that position until the tension is gone.
■ Repeat this sequence with the opposite leg.

NOTES

GLOSSARY

Abduction - in biomechanics, a movement away from the midline (center) of the body.

Accelerate - to speed up; quicken.

Actin protein - a protein localized in the I band of the myofilaments contained in the sarcomeres of muscle fibers. Acting along with the myosin protein, it is responsible for the contraction and relaxation of muscle.

Acute - having a short and relatively severe course.

Adduction - in biomechanics, a movement toward the midline of the body.

Anterior - situated in front of or in the forward part of the body; a term used in reference to the ventral or belly surface of the body.

Aponeurosis - a white, flattened or ribbon-like tendinous expansion, serving mainly to connect a muscle with the parts that it moves, e.g., the plantar aponeurosis or plantar fascial.

Articular - a term of or pertaining to a joint, e.g., articular cartilage/joint cartilage.

Articular Cartilage - a thin layer of cartilage, usually hyaline, on the articular surface of bones in synovial joints. This cartilage allows gliding motion in the joints.

Asymmetrical - lack or absence of symmetry; dissimilarity in corresponding parts or organs on opposite sides of the body which are normally alike.

Ballistic movement - a sudden, jerking movement.

Best resting length - when the myofilaments are at their longest possible length in human muscle tissue without stretching.

Biofeedback - a learned response to stimuli; in this book, learning to feel the subtlety and proper location of the tension felt in a muscle or muscle group. This is a conditioned response.

Biomechanics - the application of mechanical laws to living structures, specifically to the locomotor system of the human body.

Body mass - the total weight of the cells of the body.

Calcaneus - the heel bone.

Chondromalacia - premature degeneration of the patellar cartilage caused by chronic inflammation, causing pain when the patella is pressed against or is pulled over the femur.

Chronic - persisting over a long period of time.

Collagen - an albuminoid, a main supportive protein of skin, tendon, bone, cartilage, and connective tissue.

Collagenous fibers - fibers composed of collagen.

Concentric contraction - a shortening contraction of muscle; the muscle is expending energy and producing motion.

Contraction - as applied to muscle function it implies shortening and/or development of tension.

Current resting length - this refers to the length of the myofilaments of the weight-bearing muscles when they are not expending energy or doing work. The current resting length is seldom the best resting length in these muscles, because they shorten with repetitive usage and fatigue.

Decelerate - to slow down.

Degeneration - deterioration; change from a higher form to a lower form; especially change of tissue to a lower or less functionally active form.

Degenerative - of or pertaining to degeneration.

Dissipate - to reduce and spread, as in spreading the loading force of impact over the largest area of the articular cartilage of the joints.

Dynamic stretches - see page 74, section 2.

Eccentric capacity - this term describes the distance the myofilaments of a muscle can elongate from their *maximally contracted position* to the point where the overlapping protein fibers slightly exceed their *current resting length* during an eccentric contraction. When the overlapping protein fibers of the myofilaments slightly exceed their current resting length, the muscle spindles cause a myotatic reflex response in the muscle. This stops further elongation of the muscle. This myotatic reflex contraction stops the muscle fibers from overextending and tearing. This reflex contraction in response to loading force and myofilament elongation defines the limits of that muscle's eccentric contraction.

Eccentric contraction - an elongating contraction of muscle; the muscle is expending energy as it elongates to control motion.

Edema - swelling; an accumulation of fluid in the intercellular spaces of the body.

Elastic - susceptible of being stretched, compressed, or distorted, and then tending to assume its original shape; resilient.

Elastic deformity - as pertaining to ligaments, a tear or rupture caused by an acute or sudden overload of the structure that exceeds the structure's tensile strength.

Elastic fibers - fibers composed of the elastin protein.

Elastin - a yellow scleroprotein, the essential constituent of yellow elastic connective tissue; it is brittle when dry, but when moist is flexible and elastic.

Exostosis - a benign bony growth projecting outward from the surface of a bone.

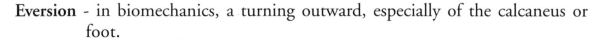

Eversion - in biomechanics, a turning outward, especially of the calcaneus or foot.

Extension - a movement which brings the bones of a limb into or toward a straight condition, e.g., extending or straightening the knee.

External - situated or occurring on the outside; many anatomical structures formerly called external are now more correctly termed lateral.

Fascia - a sheet or band of fibrous connective tissue that forms an investment for muscles and various organs of the body. Muscle fascia surrounds and contains the muscles.

Fasciculi - the large bundles of muscle fibers (myofibrils) encapsulated by individual fascial components (perimysium).

Femur - the bone that extends from the pelvis to the knee, being the longest and largest bone in the body; also called the thigh bone and femoral bone.

Fibrosis - the formation of fibrous tissue; scar tissue.

Fibula - the outer and smaller of the two bones of the lower leg below the knee. It articulates with the lateral aspect of the tibia above and the talus below (forming the lateral aspect of the ankle joint).

Flexion - the act of bending or condition of being bent, e.g., bending or flexing the knee.

Fracture - a break or rupture in a bone.

Hernia - the protrusion of a loop or knuckle of an organ or tissue through an abnormal opening.

Herniated disk - herniation of the intervertebral disk of the spine; the protrusion of the nucleus pulposus or annulus fibrosus of the disk, which may impinge on spinal nerve roots.

Hypermobility - excessive movement in a joint.

Hypertrophy - the enlargement or overgrowth of a bone due to an increase in size of its constituent cells. Bones hypertrophy in response to excess stress.

Incontinence - inability to control bowel and/or bladder functions. This can be manifested in many forms.

Inelastic - not elastic; tends not to assume its original shape if stretched or distorted; not resilient.

Inflammation - a localized protective response caused by injury or destruction of tissues. It is characterized in the acute form by pain, heat, redness, swelling, and loss of function.

Inguinal - pertaining to the groin (the inguen).

Inguinal ligament - a fibrous band of connective tissue (a ligament) running from the anterior superior spine of the ileum to the spine of the pubis. This is the largest ligament on the front of the pelvis.

Insidious - coming on in a stealthy manner; of gradual and subtle development.

Internal - situated or occurring within or on the inside; many anatomical structures formerly called internal are now correctly termed medial.

Inversion - in biomechanics, an inward movement, especially of the calcaneus and foot.

Isometric contraction - a static or holding contraction of muscle. The muscle is expending energy and maintaining a position, but the myofilaments are not changing length.

Joint capsule - articular capsule; the sac-like envelope which encloses the cavity of a synovial joint by attaching to the circumference of the articular end of each involved bone; it consists of a fibrous membrane and a synovial membrane. This capsule completely surrounds the joint itself, and functions to support the joint (the fibrous membrane), and to nourish and lubricate the joint (the synovial membrane).

Lateral - denoting a position farther from the median plane or midline of the body or of a structure; pertaining to a side.

Ligament - a band of fibrous tissue that connects bones, serving to support and strengthen joints.

Load - as used in the context of muscle stretching, e.g., loading a muscle, this term identifies the first stress placed on a muscle which results in the reflex contraction of that muscle.

Lower extremity - the leg from the hips down, including the hip, knee, ankle, and foot.

Lumbar spine - the low back, consisting of the five lumbar vertebrae between the thoracic vertebrae and the sacrum.

Macroscopic trauma - damage or injury to tissue visible with the unaided eye or without the microscope.

Malalignment - displacement out of line, especially of joint position and posture.

Medial - pertaining to the middle; closer to the midline of the body or structure.

Microscopic trauma - damage or injury to tissue visible only by the aid of the microscope.

Momentum - the quantity of motion; the product of mass times velocity.

Muscles - an organ which by contraction produces the movements of an animal organism; the contractile tissue of the body.

Myofibril - a muscle fibril, one of the slender threads which run parallel with the long axis of the fiber, and are composed of numerous myofilaments.

Myofilament - any of the ultramicroscopic threadlike structures occurring in bundles in the myofibrils of striated muscle fibers. The thick filaments are composed of myosin, the thin ones of actin; together they are responsible for the contractile properties of muscle. Two myofilaments form a sarcomere.

Myosin protein - the most abundant protein (68 per cent) in muscle, occurring chiefly in the A band of the myofilaments of the sarcomere. Acting along with actin protein, it is responsible for the contraction and relaxation of muscle.

Myotactic - pertaining to the proprioceptive senses of muscles; a contraction caused by the proprioceptors of the body in response to gravity, balance, and/or position, e.g., the myotactic reflex response of the hamstrings when bending forward from the waist. The muscle's proprioceptors, aided by other sensory organs in the body, react to gravity and balance by keeping the hamstring contracted to stabilize this posture.

Myotatic - induced by stretching or extending a muscle under load; a contraction caused or induced by stretching or extending a muscle under load, e.g., the myotatic reflex contraction of the gastrocnemius muscle when the overlapping protein fibers of the myofilaments are extended slightly past their current resting length in an eccentric contraction during the gait cycle. Also, it is the first tension (contraction) felt when a muscle is initially loaded during a stretch.

Neuron - any of the conducting cells of the nervous system.

Osgood-Schlatter disease - osteochondrosis of the tuberosity of the tibia; also called apophysitis tibialis adolescentium. This roughly translates to the fact that the patella ligament (quadriceps tendon) causes excess traction on the periosteum of the apophyseal growth plate of the anterior tibia.

Patella - a triangular sesamoid bone situated at the front of the knee in the tendon of insertion of the quadriceps muscles; the knee cap.

Patella-femoral syndrome - inflammation, pain, and degeneration of the articular surfaces of the patella and the femur (the knee cap and knee joint).

Pelvis - the lower portion of the trunk of the body, bounded anteriorly and laterally by the two hip bones and posteriorly by the sacrum and the coccyx (tail bone).

Periosteum - a specialized connective tissue covering all bones of the body, and possessing bone-forming potentialities.

Plastic deformity - as pertaining to ligaments, a continuous and prolonged stress that causes microscopic tearing, scarring, weakening, and permanent abnormal lengthening of the ligaments. This results in a loss of stability of the joint the ligaments stabilize, resulting in hypermobility of the joint.

Pliant - flexible.

Plantar fascia - bands of tendinous tissue radiating toward the bases of the toes from the medial process of the tuber calcanei (the plantar aspect of the heel bone); also called the plantar aponeurosis.

Plantar fasciitis - inflammation of the plantar fascia due to overload and *traction* that results in damage to the plantar fascia and the periosteum of the calcaneus that it arises from.

Posterior - situated in back of, or in the back part of, or affecting the back part of a structure.

Posterior compartment syndrome - damage to the deep posterior compartment of the lower leg. The compartment contains the flexor digitorum longus, flexor hallucis longus, and tibialis posterior muscles, as well as major blood vessels and nerves. Inflammation increases the pressure in this closed space, and can cause severe nerve damage.

Pronation - as applied to the foot, a combination of eversion of the calcaneus and the tarsal joints and abduction of the metatarsal joints resulting in the lowering of the medial longitudinal arch. This happens in the first part of the midstance phase of gait.

Proprioceptive - receiving nerve stimuli within the tissues of the body, as within muscles and tendons.

Proprioceptive Neuromuscular Facilitation (PNF) Stretching - see page 75, section 2.

Proprioceptor - sensory nerve terminals which give information concerning movements and position of the body; they occur chiefly in the muscles, tendons, and the labyrinth of the brain.

Propulsive phase of gait - a term used for the 4th phase of the normal gait cycle, starting when the heel is lifted off the ground, and ending when the ball of the foot leaves the ground.

Resting length of a myofilament - the position of the actin and myosin proteins in the myofilaments when the muscle is not working or expending energy.

Sacrum - the triangular bone just below the lumbar vertebrae (the lower back), formed usually by five fused vertebrae (sacral vertebrae) that are wedged dorsally between the two hip bones.

Sarcomere - the unit of length of a myofibril, being the distance between two Z bands. Two myofilaments are contained in a sarcomere.

Sciatica - a syndrome characterized by pain radiating from the lower back into the buttock and into the lower extremity (the back of the thigh) along its posterior or lateral aspect, and commonly caused by prolapse of the intervertebral disk (herniated disk); the term is also used to refer to pain anywhere along the course of the sciatic nerve.

Sciatic nerve - the largest diameter nerve in the body; it is formed by nerve roots exiting the lower spine at intervertebral levels L4, L5, S1, S2, and S3. This large nerve travels through the posterior aspect of the pelvis and down the back of the thigh. It has many branches throughout these areas.

Sesamoid - denoting a small nodular bone embedded in a tendon or joint capsule; a sesamoid bone.

Sliding elongation of muscle myofilaments - see pages 28-30, section 1.

Static - acting with mere weight without motion; not moving, not active; i.e. static stretches.

Static stretching - see page 78, section 2.

Supination - applied to the foot, a combination of inversion of the calcaneus and the tarsal joints and adduction of the metatarsals resulting in the raising of the medial longitudinal arch. This should be the second part of the midstance phase of gait.

Swelling - edema of the tissues.

Systemic - pertaining to or affecting the body as a whole.

Tendinitis (tendonitis) - inflammation of tendons and of tendon-muscle attachments.

Tendon - a fibrous cord of connective tissue in which the fibers of a muscle end and by which the muscle is attached to a bone or other structure. A tendon can only elongate 3% of the normal fiber length without rupturing.

Tendon (synovial) sheath - the sheath that surrounds tendons *anywhere* they are put under traction as they are pulled across a bony prominence. The sheath secretes synovial fluid, which serves as a lubricant as well as nourishes the tendon.

Tenosynovitis (tendosynovitis) - inflammation of a tendon sheath.

Tensile strength - relating to the strength of a tissue when tension is applied.

Tibia - the shin bone; the inner and larger bone of the leg below the knee; it articulates with the femur and head of the fibula above and with the talus below (forming the medial part of the ankle joint).

Velocity - rate of speed.

Vertebra - any of the thirty-three bones of the spinal column, comprising the seven cervical (neck), twelve thoracic (upper back), five lumbar (lower back), five sacral (posterior aspect of pelvis), and four coccygeal (tail bone) vertebrae.

Vertebrae - plural of vertebra.

Vertebral column - the spinal column; the spine.

Viscosity - a physical property of a substance that is dependent on the friction of its component molecules as they slide by one another. In general, viscosity of body tissues drops as the temperature increases, resulting in better function of those structures.

BIBLIOGRAPHY

Alter, Michael J. (1988). *Science of Stretching.* (Champaign, IL: Human Kinetics Publishers, Inc.)

Anderson, B. (1980). *Stretching.* (Bolinas, CA: Sheldon Publications).

Assussen, E. (1956). Observation on experimental muscle soreness. *Acta Rheumatology Scandinavica*, 2, 109-116.

Asmussen, E. & Bonde-Petersen, F. (1974). Storage of elastic energy in skeletal muscles in man. *Acta Physiologica Scandinavica*, 91(3), 385-392.

Basmajian, J.V. (1975). Motor learning and control. *Archives of Physical Medicine and Rehabilitation*, 58(1), 38-41.

Basmajian J.V. (1978). *Muscles Alive*, 4th ed. (Baltimore: Williams & Wilkins Co.)

Beaulieu, J.E. (1981). Developing a stretching program. *The Physician and Sportsmedicine*, 9(11), 59-69.

Boscoe, C., Tarkka, I., & Komi, P.V. (1982). Effects of elastic energy and myoelectrical potentiation of triceps surae during stretch-shortening cycle exercise. *International Journal of Sports Medicine*, 3(3), 137-140.

Bryant, S. (1984). Flexibility and stretching. *The Physician and Sportsmedicine*, 12(2), 171.

Burkett, L.M. (1970). "Causative Factors in Hamstring Injuries", *Medicine and Science in Sports,* Vol. 2, Spring 1970.

Burry, Hugh C. (1969). *"Late Effects of Neglected Soft Tissue Injury"*, Proceedings of the Royal Society of Medicine, Vol. LXII, September 1969.

Cavagna, G.A., Dusman, B., & Margaria, R. (1968). Positive work done by a previously stretched muscle. *Journal of Applied Physiology*, 24(1), 21-32.

Cavagna, G.A., Saibene, F.P., & Margaria, R. (1965). Effect of negative work on the amount of positive work performed by an isolated muscle. *Journal of Applied Physiology*, 20(1), 157-160.

Cerney, J.V. (1963). *Athletic Injuries* (Springfield, IL, Charles C. Thomas).

Ciullo, J.V., & Zarins, B. (1983). Biomechanics of the musculotendinous unit. In B. Zarins (Ed.), *Clinics in sports medicine* (Vol. 2, pp. 71-85). Philadelphia: W.B. Saunders.

Cornelius, W.L. (1983). Stretch evoked emg activity by isometric contraction and submaximal concentric contraction. *Athletic Training*, 18(2), 106-109.

Coville, C.A. (1979). Relaxation in physical education curricula. *The Physical Educator*, 36(4), 176-181.

de Vries, H.A. (1961a). Prevention of muscular distress after exercise. *Research Quarterly*, 32(2), 177-185.

de Vries, H.A. (1961b). Electromyographic observation of the effect of static stretching upon muscular distress. *Research Quarterly*, 32(4), 468-479.

de Vries, H.A. (1962). Evaluation of static stretching procedures for improvement of flexibility. *Research Quarterly*, 33(2), 222-229.

de Vries, H.A. (1966). Quantitative electromyographic investigation of the spasm theory of muscle pain. *The American Journal of Physical Medicine*, 45(3), 119-134.

Eldred, E., Hutton, R.S., & Smith, J.L. (1976). Nature of the persisting changes in afferent discharge from muscle following its contraction. *Progressive Brain Research*, 44, 157-171.

Friden, J. (1984). Changes in human skeletal muscle induced by long-term eccentric exercise. *Cell Tissue Research*, 236(2), 365-374.

Greenlaw, Robert K. (1973). *"Function of Muscles About the Hip During Normal Level Walking — An Electromyographic and Biomechanical Study."* Ph.D. thesis, Queen's University, Kingston, Canada.

Gowitzke, B.A., & Milner, M. (1980). *Understanding the scientific basis of human movement* (2nd ed.). (Baltimore: Williams & Wilkins Co.).

Grant's Atlas of Anatomy (1972). Diagram 213. (Baltimore: Williams & Wilkins Co.)

Hill, A.V. (1956). *"The Design of Muscles,"* British Medical Bulletin No. 12, p. 165.

Hill, A.V. (1961). The heat produced by a muscle after the last shock of tetanus. *Journal of Physiology* (London), 159, 518-541.

Holt, L.E. *Scientific Stretching for Sport (3-s)*. Nova Scotia: Sport Research Limited.

Holt, L.E., Travis, T.M., & Okita, T. (1970). Comparative study of three stretching techniques. *Perceptual and Motor Skills*, 21(2), 611-617.

Hough, T. (1902). Ergographic studies in muscular soreness. *The American Journal of Physiology*, 7(1), 76-92.

Janse, J. (1976). *Principles and Practice of Chiropractic*, ed. Roy M. Hildebrandt (Lombard, IL: National College of Chiropractic).

Jencks, B. (1977). *Your Body: Biofeedback at its Best*. Chicago: Nelson Hall.

Jenkins, R., & Little, R.W. (1974). A constitutive equation for parallel-fibered elastic tissue. *The Journal of Biomechanics*, 7(5), 397-402.

James, Nicholas (1970). "Injuries to Knee Ligaments", *Journal of the American Medical Association*.

Johns, R.J., & Wright, V. (1962). Relative importance of various tissues in joint stiffness. *Journal of Applied Physiology*, 17(5), 824-828.

Karpovich, P.V., & Sinning, W.E. (1971). *Physiology of Muscular Activity* (7th ed.). (Philadelphia: W. B. Saunders).

Kendall, Henry O., Kendall, Florence P., & Boynton, Dorothy (1952). *Posture and Pain* (Baltimore: Williams & Wilkins Co.)

Klein, A., Thomas, L.C. (1932). "Posture and Physical Fitness", *Body Mechanics and Practice* (New York: The Century Co.).

Laban, M.M. (1962). Collagen tissue: Implications of its response to stress in vitro. *Archives of Physical Medicine and Rehabilitation*, 43(9), 461-465.

Larson, L.A., & Michelman, H. (1973). *International Guide to Fitness and Health*. (New York: Crown Publishers).

Leard, J.S. (1984). Flexibility and conditioning in the young athlete. In L.J. Micheli (Ed.), *Pediatric and adolescent sports medicine* (194-210). (Boston: Little, Brown, and Company).

Lewin, M.D. (1944). *Backache and Sciatic Neuritis* (Philadelphia: Lea & Febiger).

Light, K.E., Nuzik, S., Personius, W., & Barstrom, A. (1984). A low-loading prolonged stretch vs high-low brief stretch in treating knee contractures. *Physical Therapy*, 64(3), 330-333.

Moore, M.A., & Hutton, R.S. (1980). Electromyographic investigation of muscle stretching techniques. *Medicine and Science in Sports and Exercise*, 12(5), 322-329.

Moorehouse, L.E., & Miller, A.T. (1971). *Physiology of Exercise*. (St. Louis: C.V. Mosby).

Retzlaff, E.W. et al. (1974). "The Piriformis Muscle Syndrome", *Journal of the American Osteopathic Association* 73: 799-807.

Sapega, A.A., Quedenfeld, T.C., Moyer, R.A., & Butler, R.A. (1981). Biophysical factors in range-of-motion exercise. *The Physician and Sportsmedicine*, 9(12), 57-65.

Schmidt, R.A., "Effects of Positional Tensioning and Stretch on Reaction Latency and Contraction Speed of Muscles", *Research Quarterly*, Vol. 38, 1967.

Schuster, R.O. (1973). *"Overuse Syndromes: Arch Strains, Heel Pains, Shin Splints"*, Annual Sports Medicine Seminar, California School of Podiatric Medicine, April 28-29, 1973.

Sheehan, George (1974). "Structural Troubles", *The Complete Runner* (Mountain View, California: World Publications).

Shy Yan Ng, "The Significance of Psoas Myospasm in the Lordotic Compared to the Kyphotic Sacro-Lumbar Spine," *Journal of the American Chiropractic Association*, Vol. 15, No. 10 (October 1978).

Slocum, D.B., James, S.L., "Biomechanics of Running", *Journal of the American Medical Association*, Vol. 205, No. 11, September 9, 1980.

Smith, J.L., Hutton, R.S., & Eldred, E. (1974). Post contraction changes in sensitivity of muscle afferents to static and dynamic stretch. *Brain Research*, 78, 193-203.

Tanigawa, M.C. (1972). Comparison of the hold-relax procedure and passive mobilization on increasing muscle length. *Physical Therapy*, 52(7), 725-735.

Taunton, J.E. (1982). Pre-game warm-up and flexibility. *The New England Journal of Sports Medicine*, 10(1), 14-18.

Verzar, F. (1963). Aging of collagen. *Scientific American*, 208(4), 104-117.

Volkov, M.V. & Mironova, Z.S. (1966). "Prophylaxis and Basic Principles of the Treatment of Trauma in Sportsmen," *"Proceedings of International Congress of Sports Sciences"* (Tokyo: Japanese Union of Sports Sciences).

Walker, S.M., "The Relation of Stretch and Temperature to Contraction of Skeletal Muscle", *American Journal of Physical Medicine*, 1959-60.

Walther, D.S. (1981). *Applied Kinesiology: Basic Procedures and Muscle Testing.* (Pueblo, CO: Systems D.C.).

Weber, S., Kraus, H. (1949). Passive and Active Stretching of Muscles, *Physiotherapy Review*, Vol. 29.

Zohar, J. (1973). Preventative Conditioning for Maximum Safety and Performance. *Scholastic Coach*, May, 1973.

NOTES

Order Form

The Stark Reality of Stretching

ALSO AVAILABLE FROM YOUR LOCAL BOOKSTORE

Canada	United States
Each copy @ $19.95 Plus GST (7%) 1.40 Total cost per book: $21.35 _____ Copies @ $21.35 CDN$_____ Shipping (1st book) $ 5.95 Add $3 for each extra book $_____ Total enclosed: CDN$_____	_____ Copies @ $17.95 US$_____ Shipping (1st book) $ 4.95 Add $3.00 for each extra book $_____ Total enclosed: US$_____

Make cheque or money order payable to:

The Stark Reality

Ship to:

Name _____

Address _____

_____

Phone (work) _____ (home) _____

The Stark Reality

Suite 1115 - 11871 Horseshoe Way, Richmond, BC Canada V7A 5H5
Local calls: (604) 538-5074 or fax: (604) 538-5063

In Canada and US call toll-free: 1-888-44STARK (1-888-447-8275)
or fax toll-free: 1-888-512-5222

Thank you for your order!

NOTES

BIOGRAPHY – DR. STEVEN D. STARK

Dr. Steven D. Stark's professional career is marked by constantly challenging old ideas in the fields of sports medicine and biomechanics. He is the first and only podiatrist in the province of British Columbia to specialize totally in sports medicine and functional control, and was the first podiatrist appointed to the Sports Medicine Council of British Columbia.

Dr. Stark opened the Podiatric Sports Medicine Group in Richmond, BC in 1986. This medical practice specializes in the treatment and prevention of injuries that are the result of biomechanical problems. His success has been based on treating patients by using a better biomechanical approach to bone malalignment and muscle imbalances and less focus on the symptomatic joint or muscle group. The response to Dr. Stark's work and his clinic has been overwhelming, attracting patients from all over Canada and the United States, and from as far away as Scotland, Chile, and Barbados. He has helped both amateur and professional athletes with correct stretching techniques that have not only helped to eliminate training errors but also improved performances and prolonged careers.

Born in New Mexico, raised in Texas, Dr. Stark holds Bachelor of Science and Doctor of Podiatric Medicine degrees. He completed a three-year postgraduate surgical residency at the David Grant USAF Medical Center at Travis Air Force Base in California. He immigrated to Canada in 1980.

Dr. Stark has been involved in sports all his life. He was an amateur and professional boxer for almost ten years with his last professional fight at The Forum in Los Angeles in 1972. He then devoted his attention to his first love, horses, becoming a professional trainer. He still spends much of his leisure time riding and training horses. He also continues to be an active swimmer, cyclist, and hiker. Dr. Stark is a firm believer that the only way to stay in shape and to continue with the activities that mean so much to him is to exercise and build good symmetrical muscle function, strength, and, most importantly, power, through stretching and flexibility.